www.rusi.org

Strategic Hedging in the Arabian Peninsula: The Politics of the Gulf–Asian Rapprochement

Jean-Loup Samaan

www.rusi.org

Royal United Services Institute for Defence and Security Studies

Strategic Hedging in the Arabian Peninsula: The Politics of the Gulf–Asian Rapprochement
First published 2018

Whitehall Papers series

Series Editor: Professor Malcolm Chalmers
Editor: Emma De Angelis

RUSI is a Registered Charity (No. 210639)
ISBN [978-0-367-10973-8]

Published on behalf of the Royal United Services Institute for Defence and Security Studies
by
Routledge Journals, an imprint of Taylor & Francis, 4 Park Square, Milton Park, Abingdon OX14 4RN

Cover Image: Chinese President Xi Jinping and his wife meet with United Arab Emirates Vice President and Prime Minister Sheikh Mohammed bin Rashid Al-Maktoum in Abu Dhabi, July 2018. *Courtesy of Xie Huanchi/PA Images*

SUBSCRIPTIONS
Please send subscription order to:

USA/Canada: Taylor & Francis Inc., Journals Department, 325 Chestnut Street, 8th Floor, Philadelphia, PA 19106 USA

UK/Rest of World: Routledge Journals, T&F Customer Services, T&F Informa UK Ltd, Sheepen Place, Colchester, Essex, C03 0LP UK

Contents

About the Author

Jean-Loup Samaan is an associate professor in strategic studies for the United Arab Emirates (UAE) National Defense College. His research focuses on Middle Eastern strategic affairs, in particular the evolution of the Gulf security system, and the Israel-Hizbullah conflict. Prior to taking up his position in the UAE, he was a researcher for the Middle East Faculty at the NATO Defense College in Rome between 2011 and 2016. He was a policy adviser at the French Ministry of Defence from 2008 to 2011. Dr Samaan has authored four books and several articles for various international academic and policy journals such as the *RUSI Journal, Survival, Orbis, Comparative Strategy, Politique Etrangère* and *Internationale Politik.*

Acknowledgements

This Whitehall Paper examines the ongoing rapprochement between Gulf and Asian states, explaining how this current trend can be characterised as a case of strategic hedging. The initial idea behind this research came to me in spring 2012 when I flew for the first time to Abu Dhabi as a NATO official. It is only then, when confronted with the physical reality of the Asian presence in the Gulf, that I started investigating the topic and writing several publications. Later, the perplexity and bewilderment with which NATO decision-makers usually responded when I made the case for a better understanding of Gulf–Asian relations definitely convinced me that there was an urgent need for a strategic analysis of the topic.

Throughout the process of writing this paper, I have been fortunate to receive support and advice from many scholars and practitioners based in the Gulf, Asia, Europe and the US. Specifically, I would like to express my gratitude to Frederic Grare, Fatiha Dazi-Heni and Jonathan Fulton, who generously took the time to review earlier drafts of the manuscripts and provided precious comments that enabled me to clarify and strengthen my argument.

Finally, I am deeply grateful for the support of the Royal United Services Institute. Malcolm Chalmers and Emma De Angelis believed in the initial proposal and supported me to turn it into a Whitehall Paper. I thank the two anonymous reviewers for their helpful and constructive comments that greatly contributed to improving this final version.

Obviously, the shortcomings of this paper are my own. The views expressed here are strictly mine and do not reflect the views of the UAE National Defense College.

List of Tables and Figures

INTRODUCTION

In 2017, commentators on Gulf politics focused most of their attention on the effects of US President Donald Trump's presidency on the region, while in fact diplomatic events in the peninsula were pointing in a different direction, demonstrating the growing strategic ties between Gulf and Asian countries.

First, Sheikh Mohammed bin Zayed Al-Nahyan, crown prince of Abu Dhabi, travelled to Delhi at the end of January, where he was invited as guest of honour to the celebration of India's Republic Day, a privilege given in the recent past to the former US and French presidents, Barack Obama and François Hollande. The event was followed by the signing of a strategic global partnership between India and the UAE, including over a dozen bilateral agreements ranging from military cooperation to investment in Indian infrastructure.[1] Four weeks later, the ruler of Saudi Arabia, King Salman, embarked on a historical month-long Asia tour that brought him to Indonesia, Brunei, Malaysia, Japan and China.[2] If economic deals were at the top of the agenda – with, for instance, $25 billion in investments contemplated in Indonesia – strategic considerations were also on the table, as Riyadh is eager to increase its counterterrorism cooperation with Muslim countries in Southeast Asia and to reinforce its Islamic Military Alliance (also known as the Islamic Military Counter Terrorism Coalition) formed on 15 December 2015.

Last, in June 2017, Saudi Arabia, alongside five other countries,[3] announced the cessation of diplomatic relations with Qatar over claims that the small emirate had been sponsoring terrorist organisations. As all eyes turned towards the US, the strongest partner of all the parties involved, the position of the US government soon appeared confused between the Department of State expressing neutrality and President Trump

---

[1] Rohan Joshi, 'Onward and Upward: India-UAE Ties', *The Diplomat*, 1 February 2017.
[2] Sholto Byrnes, 'Why King Salman's Asia Tour is so Significant', *The National*, 28 February 2017.
[3] The UAE, Yemen, Egypt, the Maldives and Bahrain.

unexpectedly endorsing the Saudi position on Twitter.[4] While Trump later backpedalled on his statement, Turkish President Recep Tayyip Erdogan announced the speeding up of the establishment of Turkey's military base in Doha, its first overseas permanent military deployment since the fall of the Ottoman Empire. Erdogan then expressed his willingness to act as a mediator.[5] The latter proposal ultimately failed, but the former enabled Qatar to counter, at least diplomatically, its sudden isolation.

These three episodes of Gulf politics may seem unrelated, but they in fact highlight one common development of regional politics: Gulf strategic partnerships are no longer exclusively looking to the US and Western, traditional powers; rather, they are moving increasingly towards other countries, particularly in Asia. This Whitehall Paper investigates this emerging trend and explains how Gulf countries have progressively been diversifying their strategic options, by 'hedging' against the risk of a US retreat and building ties with Asian powers.

The New International Relations of the Gulf

For decades, if not centuries, the Arabian peninsula was a region of the world where the distribution of power was ultimately defined by Western countries – successively Portugal, the UK and the US. As a result, Gulf monarchs were rarely depicted as strategic players that mattered. Given its geographic and demographic size and its central role in the Muslim countries, Saudi Arabia was recognised as the regional hegemon. But its diplomatic caution and limited capacities in the military field were trumped by the other regional powers that historically struggled for local hegemony: Iran and Iraq. As a matter of fact, US policy in the Gulf from President Jimmy Carter to the Iraq invasion of 2003 was to balance both Iranian and Iraqi ambitions through a posture of 'dual containment', a grand strategy later coined during the presidency of Bill Clinton, in which Saudi Arabia and its neighbours were the spectators rather than the actors of the competition.[6]

Saudi Arabia and the small, newly established Arab monarchies (UAE, Qatar, Kuwait, Oman and Bahrain) built their own Gulf Cooperation Council (GCC) in 1981, which was to create a regional order, but the operational capacity of the GCC as a provider of stability remained limited. Furthermore, successive wars (the 1980–88 Iran–Iraq War, the invasion of

---

[4] Donald J Trump, 'During my recent trip to the Middle East I stated that there can no longer be funding of Radical Ideology. Leaders pointed to Qatar – look!', @realDonalTrump Twitter account, 6 June 2017.
[5] Bulent Aras and Pinar Akpinar, *Turkish Foreign Policy and the Qatar Crisis* (Istanbul: Istanbul Policy Center, August 2017).
[6] Michael A Palmer, *Guardians of the Gulf: A History of America's Expanding Role in the Persian Gulf, 1833-1992* (New York, NY: Macmillan, 1992).

Kuwait in 1990 and the 2003 US-led invasion of Iraq) reinforced the view that Gulf states were to remain on the sideline of strategic decisions, leaving – or outsourcing – their national security to Western countries, in particular the US, the UK and France. This view of the Gulf prevailed among experts until 2011. However, this Western orientation of the Gulf security system is becoming less relevant today because of the growth of Gulf partnerships across the world, and in particular its 'pivot' towards Asia.

The geopolitics of Gulf–Asian relations is the direct result of two separate trends from the last decade. First, from the chaotic reconstruction of Iraq after the fall of Saddam Hussein to the inconsistencies of Barack Obama's policy in Syria, the unpredictability of US policy in the region has caused local actors to diversify their strategic options. Perceptions matter: whereas the Obama administration occasionally expressed its frustration regarding the lack of Gulf investment in strategic affairs, the members of the GCC grew anxious about the US's intention to leave the Middle East to pivot itself towards Asia. These concerns increased following the US decision to call for former Egyptian President Hosni Mubarak to step aside following the revolution in early 2011. They then reached a new level with the 2015 Joint Comprehensive Plan of Action (JCPOA) signed with Iran regarding its nuclear programme, which was perceived as detrimental to Gulf security.

Second, the growth of Asian economies – in particular India, China, Japan, and South Korea – is now driving oil markets. This means, by extension, that Asia's economic ties to the Gulf are becoming more consequential than those of Western powers with Arab oil producers: indeed China overtook the US as the leading consumer of Saudi oil in 2009. Since then, authorities in Riyadh, Abu Dhabi and Doha have shown increased interest in diplomatic exchanges and military cooperation through multiple official visits with not only China, but also with Japan, India and South Korea. Only a few years ago, these exchanges were dismissed as purely driven by Asian energy demands, but they have slowly started to affect the security environment of both regions, translating into bilateral partnerships that encompass strategic dialogues, common investment in advanced technology fields (such as aerospace and renewable energy), joint military exercises and counterterrorism task forces.

Emblematic of such an evolution is the frequently quoted statement of former emir of Qatar Sheikh Hamad bin Khalifa Al-Thani in March 2009: 'China is coming, India is coming, and Russia is on its way, too … I don't know if America and Europe will still be leading'.[7] The tone of his

---

[7] *Gulf Times*, 'Emir Warns of Another Iraq if Sudan Sinks into Chaos', 31 March 2009.

declaration may be blunt, but it is revealing of a narrative which is slowly emerging in the peninsula. This narrative may oversimplify the reality. It tells us that the ongoing Gulf–Asian rapprochement in all areas of bilateral cooperation would be the result of the shift in international distribution of power from the West to the East. According to this rhetoric, in the near future, the economic, military and political decline of the US and European countries would lead to their retreat from areas where they historically had influence. As far as Gulf security is concerned, this would leave the monarchies of the GCC with no other choice than to look for alternative partners, not to say security providers, among the rising powers in Asia. Hence the ongoing rapprochement between Gulf and Asian countries, particularly China and India.[8] This view of an emerging Gulf–Asian strategic nexus is partly driven by what could be characterised as geopolitical determinism or 'naturalism'.[9] In other words, it is based on the belief that Gulf and Asian countries are part of one and the same geopolitical space, made up more or less of the territories bordering the Indian Ocean, which will eventually coalesce to constitute a cohesive – and intellectually convenient– bloc. But as much as this narrative is attractive, it provides a skewed perception of the interplays in the Gulf, which does not grasp the complexity of current dynamics, nor sometimes their contradictions. Therefore, a better characterisation of this ongoing geopolitical trend is required.

The Argument

This Whitehall Paper offers a new way to look at the emerging rearrangement of power between the US, Arab monarchies and Asian countries by explaining these dynamics through the logic of 'strategic hedging' (described below). This approach allows us to debunk the two prevailing, and opposing, views of Gulf foreign affairs.

First, this paper refutes the idea of a Gulf pivot to Asia. Even though the Gulf–Asian rapprochement is significant, it does not mean a realignment of Gulf countries from the US towards Asian powers. The narrative, finding great popularity in business circles, exaggerates the

---

[8] On this narrative, see Subhash Kapila, 'The Global Power Shift to Asia: Geostrategic and Geopolitical Implications', Al Jazeera Center for Studies, 17 April 2012; Jamsheed K Choksy, 'A Sino-Persian Grab for the Indian Ocean?', *Small Wars Journal*, 7 July 2011.
[9] On this intellectual bias, see John Agnew, 'The Territorial Trap: The Geographical Assumptions of International Relations Theory', *Review of International Political Economy* (Vol. 1, No. 1, Spring 1994).

current scope of these emerging ties while understating the enduring Western presence in the Gulf.[10]

Second, this paper goes beyond the traditional view – prevailing in military circles – according to which the US remains the sole power able to shape the security environment in the peninsula.[11] In this narrative, the American military and political influence within GCC countries would be so strong that any speculation regarding lesser powers such as China, India or Russia is considered preposterous. Although this theory rightfully emphasises the upholding of a US presence in the peninsula, it overlooks many new developments in Gulf foreign policies.

Going beyond these two restricted views, this paper highlights the transitional dimension of current Gulf politics. In coming years, the international relations of Gulf states will be increasingly shaped by the following conundrum: their economic wealth will rely on the global rise of Asian powers, while their security may be sustained by military arrangements with Western countries. Against this backdrop, the paper argues that rather than a straight balancing act with regard to Washington, the much-speculated Gulf–Asian rapprochement reflects a pragmatic approach of the Gulf countries to loosen their dependency on the US and to hedge against the risk of a US retreat. In other words, Arab kingdoms are not dismissing their alliances with the US – or with other Western powers, such as the UK and France – but rather diversifying their political-security arrangements in a way that is likely to open a new era of the regional security complex – to use Barry Buzan and Ole Waever's terminology.[12]

The paper also underlines that this transitional shift is not the result of a coordinated effort by GCC members. The rapprochement with Asian powers is a regional trend in the Gulf, but it is not a common policy. Indeed, it would be misleading to assume that the GCC as a whole is hedging against a perceived decline of US power. Evidence shows that

---

[10] See the cautious and still relevant analysis of John Calabrese, 'The Consolidation of Gulf-Asia Relations: Washington Tuned in or Out of Touch?', Middle East Institute Policy Brief, No. 25, June 2009.

[11] See the past assessment that is now outdated in the military domain. Christopher Davidson, 'Persian Gulf-Pacific Asia Linkages in the 21st Century: A Marriage of Convenience?', Kuwait Programme on Development, Governance and Globalisation in the Gulf States, Working Paper, No. 7, 2010.

[12] Barry Buzan and Ole Waever define a security complex as 'a set of units whose major processes of securitisation, desecuritisation, or both are so interlinked that their security problems cannot reasonably be analysed or resolved apart from one another … The central idea remains that substantial parts of the securitisation and desecuritisation processes in the international system will manifest themselves in regional clusters'. Barry Buzan and Ole Waever, *Regions and Powers: The Structure of International Security* (Cambridge: Cambridge University Press, 2003), p. 44.

these policies remain unilateral initiatives pursued by Arab monarchies on their own. The fact that each of these countries pursues its own Asia policy is also a reflection of Gulf politics itself: it tells of the different – sometimes opposing – strategic priorities of these countries, and the low level of convergence within the GCC in the diplomatic domain. Furthermore, these policy moves are primarily conducted by four countries: Saudi Arabia; Qatar; the UAE; and to a lesser extent Oman. Although Kuwait and Bahrain cultivate ties with Asian powers, described in the following chapters, it is worth noting that the most significant policies have been conducted in Riyadh, Doha, Abu Dhabi and Muscat, where rulers have dedicated the highest level of attention to the need to diversify their strategic arrangements.

The Geopolitics of Strategic Hedging

To understand this regional development, this paper uses the concept of 'strategic hedging'. The expression 'hedging' has not yet been the topic of much scholarship in security studies. The concept is imported from financial analysis and originally refers to the idea of investing to reduce the risk of fluctuations in the price of commodities. In other words, hedging is similar to an insurance policy to cover the potential costs associated with a risk that may be encountered in the future. One of the most common ways to hedge against the probability of loss is to diversify a portfolio. It can also mean taking opposite positions in two different markets.

In the field of international relations, the concept of strategic hedging has mostly been used in the case of European and Asian security complexes, where small states may cultivate simultaneous ties with two competing powers (respectively the US and Russia, and the US and China). Evelyn Goh defines this approach as 'a set of strategies aimed at avoiding (or planning for contingencies in) a situation in which states cannot decide upon more straightforward alternatives such as balancing, bandwagoning, or neutrality'.[13] Goh's definition discusses the forms hedging strategies can

---

[13] Evelyn Goh, *Meeting the China Challenge: The U.S. in Southeast Asian Regional Security Strategies*, Policy Studies No. 16 (Washington, DC: East-West Center, 2005), p. 2. On other uses of the concept, see Robert J Art, 'Europe Hedges its Security Bets', in T V Paul, James J Wirtz and Michel Fortmann (eds), *Balance of Power: Theory and Practice in the 21st Century* (Palo Alto, CA: Stanford University Press, 2004); Eric Heginbotham and Richard J Samuels, 'Japan's Dual Hedge', *Foreign Affairs* (Vol. 81, No. 5, September/October 2002); David M Edelstein, 'Managing Uncertainty: Beliefs About Intentions and the Rise of Great Powers', *Security Studies* (Vol. 12, No. 1, Autumn 2002); Evan S Medeiros, 'Strategic Hedging and the Future of Asia-Pacific Stability', *Washington Quarterly* (Vol. 29, No. 1, Winter 2005); Mohammad

take, but it does not specify the circumstances under which a state may opt for this approach. At the systemic level, Brock Tessman argues that hedging strategies are driven by the 'deconcentration' of power in a unipolar system: it 'helps second-tier states cope with the threats and constraints they are likely to encounter under conditions of unipolarity, while simultaneously preparing them for new threats and opportunities that are likely to emerge as the system leader falls further into relative decline'.[14] If external balancing is an explicit competitive move in a regional rivalry, strategic hedging is a more prudent approach to prepare for a possible change, such as escalation with a local actor, or abandonment of an external ally. In contrast to traditional forms of foreign policy – balancing, neutrality or bandwagoning – strategic hedging reflects the volatility of the regional competition and the frailty of political alliances. But if a diversified portfolio is a coherent financial strategy, in the realm of international security its outcome is less certain. World politics remain influenced by a zero-sum game mindset and hedging means loosening the relations between two allies. As detailed in the following pages, it can engender fuzzy arrangements that may broaden the array of diplomatic options for a state in the short term, but without providing more clarity and stability to a regional security system in the long term.

Although hedging is not a new phenomenon in Europe or Asia, its emergence in the Gulf is remarkable. As explained earlier, since the establishment of modern political entities in the peninsula, the region has been under strong Western influence, with the US acting as the undisputed global power in the region since the end of the 1991 Gulf War. Admittedly, there was a degree of hedging in Gulf tendencies to balance their reliance on the US with relations with France and the UK, particularly in their selection of arms providers, but in contrast to the European and Asian continents, where countries such as Russia and China were able to challenge the American footprint, the GCC was largely perceived as a sphere of influence for Washington that did not leave space for other global powers. Therefore, put in their historical context, the ongoing developments in the region reveal a major departure from the past decades.

In this context, if the current Gulf–Asian rapprochement is not a balancing act against a hypothetical US retreat from the region, it qualifies as a hedging policy: based on the increased economic ties with China and India, Gulf leaders aim to translate these relations into new security

---

Salman, Moritz Pieper and Gustaaf Geeraerts, 'Hedging in the Middle East and China-US Competition', *Asian Politics & Policy* (Vol. 7, No. 4, October 2015).
[14] Brock F Tessman, 'System Structure and State Strategy: Adding Hedging to the Menu', *Security Studies* (Vol. 21, No. 2, Spring 2012), p. 203.

partnerships against future challenges. As in the financial analogy, these relations do not replace Gulf ties with the US, but provide insurance against the scenario of an American strategic default.

The Structure

Based on the author's research, the remainder of the paper is divided into four chapters which assess the causes, development and consequences of this Gulf hedging posture.

The first chapter offers a detailed account of the evolving Gulf security system since the end of the 1991 Gulf War. It depicts the rise and relative decline of US primacy in the peninsula. Although the US military footprint in the region remains robust and arms sales evidence the Gulf's intent to keep their forces close to the American ones, US–GCC public relations have been marked by growing tensions and suspicions, which have prompted Gulf leaders to consider diversifying their strategic bets.

The second chapter challenges the conservative view according to which Gulf–Asian economic relations are detached from strategic implications and emphasises the notion of fungibility of these trade ties. It shows how these developments involve multiple key sectors (technology, education, infrastructure and aerospace) that translate into common security interests.

The third chapter studies the 'operationalisation' of these strategic relations by looking at the politics of military cooperation in the Gulf. High-level visits between military commanders have increased, multiple defence agreements have been signed and have been followed by numerous cooperation programmes in the field of military education or joint training. Although these exchanges reflect a major diversification of Gulf military policies, it is unlikely today that any Asian country – whether China or India – could and would replace both the resources and the security guarantees provided by the US to the peninsula.

The fourth and final chapter discusses how the strategic rapprochement between Gulf and Asian countries may eventually be impeded by the way it impacts – and is impacted by – local competition. For instance, it is not clear how Gulf countries that historically have had a strong military relationship with Pakistan could strengthen their strategic dialogue with India without challenging their ties to the former. Therefore, the hedging approach leads both Gulf and Asian powers to adopt a cautious position and to depict their initiatives as cooperative but not targeting any common competitor or rival. In other words, they try to avoid being trapped in the classic zero-sum game of alliances, a position that might not be sustainable in the long term.

I. THE END OF THE POST-GULF WAR ORDER

This chapter looks at the modern evolution of the Gulf security system, and in particular the way the recent development in US Middle East policy is signalling the end of the current structure of the regional order. The historical perspective underlines two realities that are too often neglected. First, the current security architecture of the Gulf is not an old construct. Relying primarily on US military presence, this loose structure can be traced back to the 1991 Gulf War and the subsequent reinforcement of US troops in the region. Second, these US deployments may have been massive, but they did not prevent frequent misperceptions and diplomatic tensions between Washington and Gulf capitals regarding the former's resolve to defend its partners in the region.

The Origins of US Primacy in the Gulf

US primacy in the region is frequently assumed to have started a long time ago, following the much-discussed meeting between US President Franklin D Roosevelt and Saudi Arabia's King Ibn Saud on board the USS *Quincy* on 20 February 1945, but viewing this date as a historical turning point is a bit excessive.[1]

Admittedly, by 1945 the US was replacing the declining British Empire and the American engineers of Standard Oil of California had been exploring an oil concession from Saudi Aramco, Saudi Arabia's state-owned oil firm, since 1933. But for many years, US administrations remained reluctant to militarily replace the British and to fully endorse security responsibilities in this remote part of the world. Arguably, the US military became the 'guardians of the Gulf' only after it was left with no choice, following the 'East of Suez' withdrawal of British forces ordered by Britain's Prime Minister Harold Wilson in 1968.[2] Even after the British retreat, Washington

---

[1] Thomas W Lippman, 'The Day FDR Met Saudi Arabia's Ibn Saud', *The Link* (Vol. 38, No. 2, April/May 2005).
[2] Palmer, *Guardians of the Gulf*, p. 40.

cautiously avoided playing the role of an equal substitute. For a while, diplomats at the US Department of State discussed building a NATO-style organisation for the Gulf that would rely on Saudi Arabia and the Shah's Iran.[3] A close US ally at that time, Tehran was perceived as a pivotal state that could allow the Americans to not deploy too many of their own forces in the Gulf. In December 1977, President Jimmy Carter declared in a speech that 'Iran, because of the great leadership of the Shah, is an island of stability in one of the more troubled areas of the world'.[4] However, the initial plan was short-lived: the Shah remained suspicious of any US grand scheme for the region, while the US decision-makers questioned the reliability of the Iranian leader, whose authoritarian style reflected preoccupying 'megalomaniac' tendencies' for the US intelligence community.[5] In this context, Iran refused in 1968 to host a US naval regional base, which led the US Navy to discuss the project with the small Kingdom of Bahrain on the other side of the Gulf.[6] In 1971, as British forces were leaving its capital, Manama, the US Navy – which had been operating a small detachment since the Second World War – merely replaced them.

The following decade, the US footprint in the Gulf increased as a result of the unfolding of the Iran–Iraq War. On 1 January 1983, the United States Central Command (CENTCOM) was born, whose area of responsibility included, at that time, nineteen countries.[7] As the conflict between Tehran and Baghdad extended, it soon moved offshore and disrupted trade sea lanes. As the Gulf kingdoms supported Saddam Hussein – primarily out of fear of Iranian hegemonic aspirations over the Muslim world – Iranian forces started targeting ships crossing the Strait of Hormuz. Contemplating the risk of economic disruption caused by this maritime escalation, the administration of US President Ronald Reagan decided to deploy air and naval assets to secure the strait. In 1986, the tanker war – during which Iran targeted Kuwaiti and Saudi ships crossing the Strait – led Gulf states to urge the Americans to intervene.

It is now known from the declassified archives of the Reagan administration that although the US Navy eventually responded by

---

[3] *Ibid.*, p. 52.
[4] Jimmy Carter, 'Tehran, Iran Toasts of the President and the Shah at a State Dinner', 31 December 1977, <http://www.presidency.ucsb.edu/ws/?pid=7080>, accessed 12 April 2018.
[5] Roham Alvandi, *Nixon, Kissinger, and the Shah: The United States and Iran in the Cold War* (New York, NY: Oxford University Press, 2014), p. 152.
[6] Jeffrey Macris, *The Politics and Security of the Gulf: Anglo-American Hegemony and the Shaping of a Region* (London: Routledge, 2010), p. 177.
[7] Amitav Acharya, *U.S. Military Strategy in the Gulf: Origins and Evolution Under the Carter and Reagan Administrations* (London: Routledge, 1989), p. 126.

reflagging the ships, the decision was in fact less about strengthening the US position in the Gulf than about preventing USSR interference.[8] As soon as the Iran–Iraq War ended in 1988, the Americans quickly reduced their naval presence with the intention to preserve the status quo and keep their distance from the region. However, on 2 August 1990, the Iraqi invasion of Kuwait jeopardised this US posture and eventually triggered an international reaction that would completely change the regional security environment.

The Impact of the 1991 Gulf War on the Peninsula Security Architecture

By the winter of 1990, 200,000 American soldiers were sent to Saudi Arabia to conduct Operation *Desert Shield* to protect the country against a potential Iraqi invasion. While the subsequent Operation *Desert Storm* quickly crushed the Iraqi forces, the images of the Kuwaiti royal family fleeing the country left a lasting impact on the rulers of the GCC and fuelled their fears of regime collapse. As a result, the post-1991 security architecture saw a reinforcement of bilateral ties between the individual Gulf monarchies on the one hand, and Western powers – the US, the UK and France – on the other, through a multitude of defence agreements and security guarantees. These Western-oriented security policies reflected the limitations of a local response to the security challenges facing the Gulf. Since its birth in 1981, the GCC had been slow in its various attempts to build an indigenous regional security system. Its members remained cautious about the principle of mutual solidarity. There was no article in the original GCC Charter similar to the famous Article 5 of the North Atlantic Treaty that epitomised collective defence.[9] Moreover, back in the

---

[8] This is the analysis supported by Reagan's Secretary of Defense Caspar Weinberger in his memoirs. Caspar Weinberger, *Fighting for Peace: Seven Critical Years in the Pentagon* (New York, NY: Grand Central Publishing, 1990), p. 388.

[9] Article 5 of the North Atlantic Treaty states that 'The Parties agree that an armed attack against one or more of them in Europe or North America shall be considered an attack against them all and consequently they agree that, if such an armed attack occurs, each of them, in exercise of the right of individual or collective self-defence recognised by Article 51 of the Charter of the United Nations, will assist the Party or Parties so attacked by taking forthwith, individually and in concert with the other Parties, such action as it deems necessary, including the use of armed force, to restore and maintain the security of the North Atlantic area. Any such armed attack and all measures taken as a result thereof shall immediately be reported to the Security Council. Such measures shall be terminated when the Security Council has taken the measures necessary to restore and maintain international peace and security'. For a recent analysis of the strategic implications of Article 5, see Bruno Tertrais, 'Article 5 of the Washington

1990s, GCC members were still arguing with each other over territorial disputes. Saudi Arabia and Qatar engaged in a brief confrontation in 1992 at their border that led to the death of a Saudi sheikh and two Qatari soldiers. The Hawar Islands were contested by both Qatar and Bahrain, while the Al-Buraimi Oasis remained the object of tensions between Saudi Arabia and the UAE.[10]

Additionally, Gulf armed forces were only nascent institutions at that time, with investment in national militaries only being triggered by the invasion of Kuwait. Notably, the Defence Forces of the Emirate of Dubai only joined the UAE Federal Armed Forces in 1997.

In this context, security relations with the US were the cornerstone to ensuring the survival of local regimes. By 1992, Doha had signed a defence and security agreement with Washington and in the following decade, the country became the location of the forward headquarters of CENTCOM. Similarly, in Bahrain, the US naval base was expanded and in 1995 renamed the United States Fifth Fleet. From Washington's point of view, its role as security provider was dictated by the imperatives of economic stability. A crisis in the Gulf could affect oil prices and by extension, the US and global economies. As shown in Figure 1, US imports from GCC countries of crude oil steadily increased during the 1990s, increasing from 597,629 thousand barrels in 1993 to a peak of 972,479 thousand barrels in 2001.[11]

Although the Clinton administration postulated a 'dual containment' approach (containing Iraq and Iran) as its regional strategy for the Gulf, the operational implications of the policy were not evident. Whereas the economic and political isolation of Saddam Hussein severely weakened the Iraqi ruler, the containment of Iran was less effective. The presidency of Iran's Mohammad Khatami (1997–2005) even witnessed a momentum for détente that triggered disappointment in Gulf capitals, in particular Riyadh, due to the US's perceived accommodating attitude towards Iran.[12] And the later revelations in 2003 of Iran's clandestine nuclear programme only reinforced Gulf perceptions of the Clinton administration's leniency towards Tehran.

Treaty: Its Origins, Meaning and Future', *NATO Defense College Research Paper* (No. 130, April 2016).

[10] J E Peterson, 'Sovereignty and Boundaries in the Gulf States: Settling the Peripheries', in Mehran Kamrava (ed.), *International Politics of the Persian Gulf* (Syracuse, NY: Syracuse University Press, 2011), pp. 21–49.

[11] Official data gathered by the US Energy Information Administration (EIA), <https://www.eia.gov/dnav/pet/hist/LeafHandler.ashx?n=PET&s=MCRIMUSPG1&f=A>, accessed 4 September 2017.

[12] Neil Partrick (ed.), *Saudi Arabian Foreign Policy: Conflict and Cooperation* (London: I B Tauris, 2016), p. 359.

Figure 1: US Imports by Country of Origin

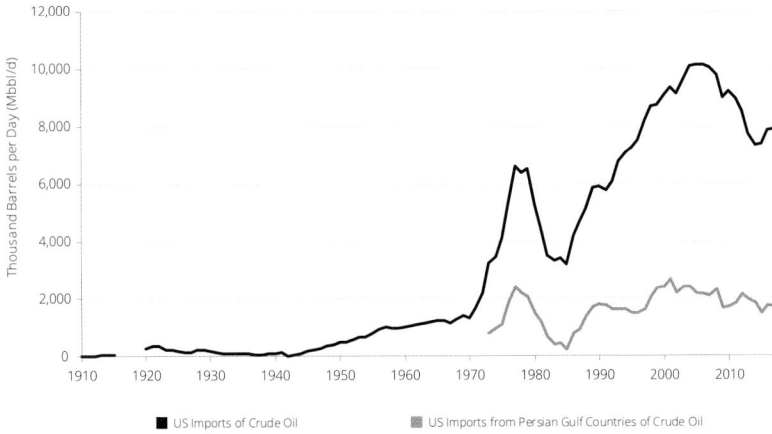

Source: US Energy Information Administration, 'Petroleum and Other Liquids'.

However, the dual containment strategy was suddenly moved to the background in 2001 with the 9/11 attacks. These attacks directly put the relevance of US Gulf policy into question: whereas for decades, the US military had been sending troops to defend these Arab kingdoms, US citizens were discovering that fifteen Saudis and two Emiratis were among the nineteen terrorists that conducted the attacks. The policy debate that ensued was heated: in 2002, a leaked briefing to the Defense Policy Board stated that 'Saudi Arabia supports our enemies and attacks our allies'.[13] Although the Department of Defense quickly distanced itself from the statement, it reflected the level of tension that was now surrounding US–Gulf relations. As a result, in the following decade the US government revised its import policy to decrease reliance on Gulf oil: in May 2003 the US imported 69,549 thousand barrels of Saudi oil per month, but by August 2009 this had fallen to 21,912 thousand.[14] If the US–Saudi partnership had looked like a marriage of convenience, the relationship was now turning into a political liability in Washington.

The Growth of US Unpredictability

If the US military presence in the Gulf were to provide stability and ensure the uninterrupted flow of energy supplies from the region to the world, the

---

[13] Thomas E Ricks, 'Briefing Depicted Saudis as Enemies', *Washington Post*, 6 August 2002.
[14] Official data gathered by the US EIA, <https://www.eia.gov/dnav/pet/hist/LeafHandler.ashx?n=pet&s=mcrimussa1&f=m>, accessed 4 September 2017.

political events that followed the 9/11 attacks questioned the stabilising factor of US policy in the region. The 2003 Iraq War was the next turning point in the complex relationship between the US and the Gulf.

As the Pentagon prepared for the invasion, emirs and monarchs of the Arab Peninsula found themselves in a delicate situation. On the one hand, the removal of Saddam Hussein, the Iraqi leader that had invaded one GCC member while openly defying the Saudi kingdom, was welcomed, while on the other, the neo-conservative rhetoric that shaped the 2003 invasion as a 'regime change' operation to promote the freedom agenda of President George W Bush's administration in the Middle East was at odds with the authoritarian regimes of Gulf rulers. To comply with US demands, promises were made by Gulf leaders to hold local elections, and institutional reforms were launched to provide a space for parliaments in the political process. The results were frequently mixed and slow.[15]

Soon it was the absence of a clear US plan for the post-Saddam reconstruction of Iraq that puzzled the Gulf neighbours, in particular Kuwait and Saudi Arabia. Both countries anxiously eyed the civil war ensuing in the country next to their border. The new regime emerging in Baghdad and led by Prime Minister Nouri Al-Maliki after 2006 only exacerbated these Gulf anxieties. Maliki soon pursued a sectarian agenda that favoured his entourage, mostly from the Shia community, while moving the Sunni population to the fringe. Moreover, Maliki's policies strengthened the influence of Iran in Baghdad.[16] By December 2011, as the US officially launched its military withdrawal from Iraq, Gulf leaders were observing a problematic situation: the US was leaving an Iraqi national military that was barely functional and giving free rein to a government that allowed Iran to accumulate more power in the region.[17] This withdrawal would become one of many episodes during the presidency of Barack Obama that reinforced the idea in the Gulf that Washington was tired of the region and would leave it as soon as possible.

A month before, in November 2011, the US government announced its 'pivot' to Asia, causing as much anxiety in the Gulf as in Europe.[18] The

---

[15] Fatiha Dazi-Héni, *Monarchies et sociétés d'Arabie: Le temps des confrontations* (Paris: Presses de Sciences Po, 2006), p. 33.

[16] Toby Dodge, *Iraq: From War to a New Authoritarianism*, Adelphi Series No. 434–35 (London: Routledge, 2012).

[17] Jeffrey Martini et al., *The Outlook for Arab Gulf Cooperation* (Santa Monica, CA: RAND Corporation, 2016), p. ix.

[18] Author's interviews with national security officials in Kuwait City, Abu Dhabi and Doha, 2012.

'pivot' was first and foremost a narrative built by the US administration to move on from the War on Terror and its military adventures in Iraq and Afghanistan, which had consumed a tremendous amount of defence expenditure over the last decade. It also took stock of the evolving world order, with Asian power plays emerging as the future centre of gravity of US global commitment. But, like their European counterparts, Gulf leaders feared that in a world of limited resources, the 'pivot' meant less political attention and fewer troops to protect their region. In fact, if the initial statements from the Obama administration emphasised the role of Asia in the twenty-first century, the official documents that followed toned down the rhetoric. In its strategic guidance of January 2012, the US Department of Defense stated that stability in the Gulf remained a core US national security interest, even though it clearly stated that the US 'will of necessity rebalance toward the Asia-Pacific region'.[19]

For GCC countries, the most problematic part of the American discourse was the fact that this 'pivot' to Asia emerged at the same time as Washington expressed its intention to 'engage' with all Gulf states, including Iran. After his election in 2008, President Obama argued for a new framework of negotiations with the Iranian leadership. In the nuclear field, this meant challenging the previous Western demand for the suspension of nuclear enrichment – a provision included in the Non-Proliferation Treaty – as a precondition for talks. In March 2009, Obama sent a message marking the Iranian New Year (*Nowruz*) – the first time a US president had publicly addressed the Islamic Republic of Iran – in which he called for 'engagement that is honest and grounded in mutual respect'.[20] Eventually, Obama's approach proved inconclusive: the nuclear talks were still lingering; Iran's regional policy was becoming more assertive; and internal opposition was severely crushed in 2009. But the engagement phase with Iran compounded Gulf states' anxieties and substantiated local fears that US regional actions might actually become a liability for the survival of the regimes.

Eventually, these Gulf–US tensions reached their height during the 2011 Arab uprising and in particular the White House's position in the last days of Mubarak's presidency. Following events in Tunisia, Egypt experienced massive demonstrations in January 2011 that called for the removal of its ruler. The US government not only embraced the calls for democracy from the protesters, but diplomats directly discussed with Egyptian officials plans for a Mubarak resignation, followed by a

---

[19] US Department of Defense, 'Sustaining US Global Leadership: Priorities for 21st Century Defense', January 2012, p. 2. Emphasis in original.
[20] *The Guardian*, 'Barack Obama's Address to Iran', 20 March 2009.

transitional government.[21] The swift turn from the US government towards a post-Mubarak Egypt embarrassed those Gulf monarchies that had been close supporters of the Egyptian president.[22] First, the GCC rulers considered the US's casual abandonment of a 30-year ally to be a concrete reflection of Washington's absence of solidarity with its allies in times of crisis. In other words, they feared that if faced with similar protests in their own countries, Washington would not hesitate in favouring regime change. Second, the US's public support of the elected government of Mohamed Morsi, affiliated with the Muslim Brotherhood, was understood as an endorsement of a political actor – the Brotherhood – which was identified by countries such as Saudi Arabia and the UAE as a direct threat to their own regimes. The American position would be quickly equated to support for the Muslim Brotherhood. Therefore, two years later, the military takeover of Egypt was welcomed by both Saudi Arabia and the UAE, whereas voices in Washington were more confused and expressed fears of a return to authoritarianism.[23]

The US treatment of the crisis in Bahrain also increased resentment. As discussed earlier, Manama had been a historical location for US forces in the peninsula. Despite the growing unrest there, speculation over the relocation of the US Navy base was systematically dismissed by Pentagon officials, although the Obama administration 'held up some new weapons sales to Bahrain and curtailed U.S. assistance to Bahrain's internal security organizations led by the Ministry of Interior'.[24] This US restraint regarding the Bahraini regime directly contradicted the GCC response to events in Manama: soon after the beginning of the 2011 uprising, the GCC approved Manama's request for troops to support its security response. A joint Peninsula Shield Force (the military arm of the GCC), led by Saudi Arabia, was built up in March 2011. It included 1,200 Saudi armed forces and 600 UAE police.[25] In addition, Kuwait sent naval forces to strengthen Bahrain's maritime borders. The Obama administration opposed this GCC intervention and advised the Bahraini leadership to meet the demands of protesters for political reform. Although neither Obama nor any of his

---

[21] Helene Cooper and Mark Landler, 'White House and Egypt Discuss Plan for Mubarak's Exit', *New York Times*, 3 February 2011.

[22] In his memoirs, Robert Gates, former secretary of defense (2006–11), shares details of his exchanges with Gulf rulers warning him of the danger of seeing a 'new Iran' in Egypt. Robert M Gates, *Duty: Memoirs of a Secretary at War* (New York, NY: Vintage, 2014), p. 468.

[23] Dan Roberts, 'US in Bind Over Egypt After Supporting Morsi but Encouraging Protesters', *The Guardian*, 3 July 2013.

[24] Kenneth Katzman, 'Bahrain: Reform, Security, and U.S. Policy', Congressional Research Service, 7-5700, 5 June 2018, Summary.

[25] *Ibid.*, p. 5.

administration openly supported the removal of the Khalifa regime, criticism of its security response to the protests increased in Washington.[26]

At the military level, US–Bahrain relations were not affected, although contingency plans were now openly discussed. For instance, in May 2015, the House of Representatives passed a defence bill asking the Pentagon to review plans for a potential relocation of the Fifth Fleet if the crisis in Manama were to escalate.[27] Asked by the press, the congressman behind the call, Hank Johnson, explained that '[t]he reason that we have to do some planning now for that contingency is exactly because of the Bahraini monarchy's failure to address the concerns of the people'.[28] This reinforced the view within the GCC that the US government, at least under Obama, was not taking its political commitments seriously, and that security guarantees would hold only as long as they were not put to the test.[29]

Finally, the 2015 nuclear deal with Iran, the JCPOA, confirmed the long-held suspicions in the GCC that the US administration was searching for accommodation with the regime in Tehran. The revelation of secret talks between the Americans and the Iranians being facilitated by Oman provided a conspiratorial flavour that nurtured the rising belief that the Obama administration had been shifting its alliance from the Gulf to Iran. For local observers, the combination of Iran's interference in Bahrain through its support of the Shia protesters and the US move away from the Khalifa regime in Manama indicated that there was a clear US–Iran understanding regarding the peninsula.[30]

In this context, it should come as no surprise that virulent anti-American speeches flourished in the region, even from high-level officials. For instance, in January 2012, the Dubai Chief of Police, Dhahi Khalfan Tamim, affirmed during a public conference that U.S. policy In the region is the number one security threat [to the Gulf].[31] Although his speech was not endorsed by Emirati authorities, it reflected a certain frustration among the local elites. Similarly, Obama's last visit to Saudi Arabia in April 2016 indicated the extent of the degradation of the bilateral relationship. The American president was greeted at the airport 'only' by the governor of

---

[26] *Ibid.*, p. 13.

[27] 'National Defense Authorization Act for Fiscal Year 2016 (US)', 2015.

[28] Julian Pecquet, 'Bahrain Bristles as U.S. Threatens to Move Fleet', *US News*, 19 May 2015.

[29] Author's interviews with Gulf officials, spring 2015.

[30] Author's interview with a high-ranking official from Bahrain Defence Force, Manama, December 2013.

[31] MEMRI, 'Dubai Police Chief Dahi Khalfan Tamim: "U.S. Policy Is the No. 1 Security Threat" to the Gulf States; America Has "Realized the Dreams Of Iran" in Iraq, "Is Now Embracing" the Muslim Brotherhood, and "Is No Longer An Ally"', Special Dispatch No. 4468, 31 January 2012.

Riyadh, Prince Faisal bin Bandar Al-Saud, and his arrival was not even broadcast live on the official Saudi TV channel.[32]

In addition to the multiple disagreements between the two countries, the Obama visit was affected by the Justice Against Sponsors of Terrorism Act (JASTA),[33] which was going under review by the Senate at the same time. According to its provisions, JASTA authorised federal courts to exercise jurisdiction over a foreign country and to charge it with support for acts of international terrorism against US citizens. In practice, the new legislation enabled families of victims of the 9/11 attacks to continue a lawsuit against the government of Saudi Arabia for its alleged support of the attacks. Although this legislation was unlikely to lead to concrete results, it added a final layer of distrust between Washington and Riyadh as President Obama's term of office was nearing its end.

A Trump–Gulf Honeymoon?

In contrast with the perplexity and shock provoked in Europe by the election of Donald Trump as president of the US in November 2016, the result was more positively welcomed in the Arabian Peninsula. First, it put an end to the chapter of the Obama presidency that had been largely perceived as detrimental to Gulf interests. But the election of Trump also led to commonalities in the assessment of security priorities between the new administration in Washington and the GCC members, in particular Saudi Arabia and the UAE.

Trump had been extremely vocal about his aversion to Obama's Iran policy. In his unique inflammatory style, he described the JCPOA as 'one of the most incompetent contracts I've ever seen … I've never seen more of a one-sided deal, I think, in my life'.[34] After entering the White House, Trump sent confused messages on the agreement, admitting at first that Iran was complying with the JCPOA and then threatening to 'decertify' the deal itself. Eventually, he announced in early May 2018 that he was terminating the US participation in the JCPOA, and as a result, reimposing sanctions that had been lifted by the 2015 agreement.[35] As a matter of fact, he had already initiated two rounds of economic sanctions (in February and July 2017) targeting Iranian companies involved in the production of Iran's

---

[32] Ian Black, 'Obama's Chilly Reception in Saudi Arabia Hints at Mutual Distrust', *The Guardian*, 20 April 2016.
[33] 'Justice Against Sponsors of Terrorism Act 2016 (US)'.
[34] Max Fisher, 'We Painstakingly Annotated Donald Trump's Strange and Revealing Foreign Policy Interview', *Vox*, 4 September 2015.
[35] White House, 'President Donald J. Trump is Ending United States Participation in an Unacceptable Iran Deal', Fact Sheet, 8 May 2018, <https://www.whitehouse.gov/briefings-statements/president-donald-j-trump-ending-united-states-participation-unacceptable-iran-deal/>, accessed 9 May 2018.

Table 1: US Military Footprint in the Gulf

Country	Type of Deployment	Military Personnel	Capabilities
Bahrain	HQ Fifth Fleet	5,000	Patriot PAC-2/3 Air Defence; 1 CVN; 1 SSGN; 1 SSN; 3 CGHM; 4 DDGHM; 1 DDGM; 1 LSD; 10 PCFG
Kuwait	CENTCOM (Army Component)	13,000 (Army Brigade)	Patriot PAC-2/3 Air Defence
Qatar	CENTCOM (Forward HQ)	8,000	1 bbr sqn; 2 ISR sqn; 2 tkr sqn; Patriot PAC-2/3 Air Defence
Saudi Arabia	CENTCOM (detachment)	400	Education and Training
UAE	CENTCOM (detachment)	5,000	1 ftr sqn; 1 FGA sqn; 1 ISR sqn; 1 AEW&C sqn; 1 tkr sqn; 1 ISR UAV sqn; Patriot PAC-2/3 Air Defence

Note: CVN: aircraft carrier with nuclear propulsion; SSGN: conventional missile submarine; SSN: attack submarine with nuclear propulsion; CGHM: cruiser, guided missile, hanger facilities, anti-ship missiles; DDGHM: destroyer, guided missile, hanger facilities, anti-ship missiles; DDGM: destroyer, guided missile, anti-ship missiles; LSD: landing craft carrier; PCFG: fast patrol craft missiles; bbr sqn: bomber squadron; ISR sqn: intelligence, surveillance and reconnaissance squadron; tkr sqn: tanker squadron; ftr sqn: fighter squadron; FGA sqn: fighter ground attack squadron; AEW&C sqn: airborne early warning and control squadron.
Source: International Institute for Strategic Studies, *The Military Balance 2017* (London: Routledge, 2017); Congressional Research Service.

ballistic missiles. More broadly, Trump and his administration have embraced a view of Iranian regional policy that echoes the prevailing view in the Arabian Peninsula. In particular, his administration has condemned Iran for its support to the Houthi rebels in Yemen, where a Saudi-led coalition has been conducting a military campaign since 2015.[36]

The Trump presidency also meant a change for countries that had been under the scrutiny of the previous administration. In March 2017, only a few weeks into his new role, then Secretary of State Rex Tillerson indicated that the US administration would lift the restrictions imposed by Obama on the sale of US fighter jets and other arms to Bahrain.[37] The past rhetoric on sales being conditional on progress made with regard to political reforms and human rights seemed to have gone. Similarly, Trump's public support of Egypt's President Abdel Fattah Al-Sisi also aligned with the Saudi–Emirati position. The visit of the Egyptian ruler to

---

[36] White House, Office of the Press Secretary, 'Statement by President Donald J. Trump on Yemen', 6 December 2017; White House, Office of the Press Secretary, 'White House Statement on Iranian-Supported Missile Attacks Against Saudi Arabia', 8 November 2017.
[37] Molly Hennessy-Fiske, 'Why Gulf Arab Leaders are Welcoming Trump's Transactional Foreign Policy', *Los Angeles Times*, 19 May 2017.

Washington in spring 2017 included a carefully orchestrated meeting in the Oval Office to demonstrate the proximity between Al-Sisi and Trump. During the visit, the latter reassured Al-Sisi of the US commitment to annual military aid and emphasised the importance of fighting extremism and terrorism in a way that clearly echoed the contemporary Egyptian narrative. This was in stark contrast to Obama's personal restraint towards Al-Sisi and his administration's dilemmas regarding the provision of US aid to the Egyptian regime. Trump's embrace of Al-Sisi was in line with his views on the Middle East: during his election campaign, his foreign policy advisers such as former National Security Advisor Michael Flynn or the controversial right-wing scholar Walid Phares designated Iran and the Muslim Brotherhood as the biggest threats in the region.[38] This assessment converged with the views in Riyadh and Abu Dhabi, where the Brotherhood is identified as a terrorist organisation.

The warming up of US–Gulf relations culminated in Trump's visit to Saudi Arabia in May 2017. The lavish reception offered by the Saudi king to the American president was a remarkable shift from Obama's last visit.[39] It reflected the personalised dimension of the relations between Trump and Gulf leaders and the high expectations they had of the new incumbent in the White House.

Nevertheless, the idea of a Gulf–Trump honeymoon may be overhyped. First, during Trump's election campaign, Gulf leaders seemed to voluntarily ignore his rhetoric, in the name of pragmatism. But if Obama as a president was cautious in his commitments to the GCC, Trump was reckless. When asked about Saudi Arabia in August 2015, Trump confessed that he 'wasn't a big fan'.[40] With regard to the security commitments made by the US to the kingdom, he argued that Saudi Arabia 'is going to be in big trouble pretty soon and they're going to need help … We get nothing for it and they're making a billion dollars a day … the primary reason we're with Saudi Arabia is because we need the oil. Now we don't need the oil so much'.[41] In addition, Trump's overt anti-Muslim comments made during his campaign, in particular following his call to ban Muslims from entering the US, triggered outrage from both Gulf investors and leaders. The GCC even issued a common statement to share its 'deep concern at the increase of hostile, racist and

---

[38] Eli Lake, 'Trump's Coming Witch Hunt Against Political Islam', *Bloomberg*, 30 November 2016.
[39] Anne Applebaum, 'Trump's Bizarre and Un-American Visit to Saudi Arabia', *Washington Post*, 21 May 2017.
[40] Sultan Al Qassemi, 'What a Trump Presidency Means for the Gulf', Middle East Institute, 25 February 2016.
[41] *Ibid.*

inhumane rhetoric against refugees in general and Muslims in particular'.[42] After the final results of the election were released, Gulf leaders dismissed Trump's comments as ill-tempered political speeches during a US presidential campaign, but in doing so they underestimated how much this rhetoric reflected the platform on which Trump ran, as well as his electoral base, which he would need to keep to aim for a second mandate in 2020. In other words, Trump's foreign policy is first and foremost an extension of his political campaign at home.

The fact that Trump went from this negative rhetoric to a somewhat more positive view of the Gulf and Saudi Arabia could be seen as proof of his pragmatism, but it could also underline his inconsistencies and unreliability. For instance, after months expressing strong support for the Saudi-led coalition in Yemen, Trump issued an official statement on 6 December 2017 calling on the leadership of Saudi Arabia to 'completely allow food, fuel, water, and medicine to [immediately] reach the Yemeni people who desperately need it'.[43] The sudden shift and the peremptory tone of the statement had obviously not been anticipated by Gulf officials.[44]

With regard to US aid to Egypt, the Trump administration surprisingly decided in August 2017 to delay $195 million in military funding while denying another $95.7 million due to 'concerns over Egypt's human rights record and its cozy relationship with North Korea'.[45] The sums were modest in comparison to the overall amount of US aid to Egypt and Trump later stated that his government would consider resuming it, but this clearly underlined a gap between the public display of support to Al-Sisi during his visit to Washington and the decisions taken a few months later.[46]

Trump's handling of the Qatar crisis of 2017 also exemplifies this issue. Although discontent between Saudi Arabia and Qatar had been looming for several years, the fast escalation of the crisis took the US by surprise. It put Washington in a delicate situation as it had signed bilateral agreements with all parties involved and its troops were deployed in most of these countries.

In that context, Washington had nothing to win with this crisis. Therefore, the first official reaction, conveyed by Tillerson, was extremely

---

[42] *Ibid.*

[43] White House, 'Statement by President Donald J. Trump on Yemen'.

[44] Missy Ryan and Josh Dawsey, 'Why Trump Lashed out at Saudi Arabia About its Role in Yemen's War', *Washington Post*, 29 December 2017.

[45] Gardiner Harris and Declan Walsh, 'U.S. Slaps Egypt on Human Rights Record and Ties to North Korea', *New York Times*, 22 August 2017.

[46] *Reuters*, 'U.S. Will Consider Resuming Halted Military Aid to Egypt: Trump', 20 September 2017.

cautious. Tillerson encouraged 'the parties to sit down together' and reminded them that 'it is important that the GCC remain unified'.[47] This initial attempt to de-escalate the dispute was followed a day later by two tweets from Trump which endorsed the accusations made by Saudi Arabia and the UAE and demanded that Qatar comply with the claims. The tweets created confusion: what was the official US position between Tillerson's statement and Trump's social network posts? If Trump was explicitly condemning Qatar, what did it imply for the US commitment to the emirate and its military presence? A day later, Trump appeared to backpedal as he spoke to Qatar's Emir Tamim bin Hamad Al-Thani and 'offered to help the parties resolve their differences, including through a meeting at the White House if necessary'.[48] The US government was back to a neutral position and in the following days, US–Qatar working relations continued as usual. On 23 June 2017, then White House Press Secretary Sean Spicer also de-emphasised the importance of the crisis by qualifying the dispute as 'a family issue' that GCC members 'should work out'.[49] If the eventual position of the Trump administration was a traditional one calling for Gulf unity, the initial one expressed through the president's tweet was unprecedented in its form and content. For countries that had been supportive of the new American leader, this underlined the level of unpredictability of current US foreign policy.

A US president who likes to portray himself as a businessman-turned-president, a 'transactional' leader and deal-maker that always thinks 'America First' may not be without consequences for Gulf investments in the US. Officials in the UAE still remember the 2006 controversy stirred by the US Congress over Dubai Ports World and its management contracts of six ports in the US, which was considered a potential security issue and eventually forced the Emirati company to turn over the operation to US contractors. More recently, it is worth considering the financial losses of the three major Gulf airlines – Dubai's Emirates, Abu Dhabi's Etihad and Qatar's Qatar Airways. In July 2017, Etihad announced a $1.9-billion loss for 2016 while Emirates's profits plunged 82.5 per cent in the same year.[50] There are various reasons for these losses (falling oil prices and a decrease in the European tourism sector, among others), but Trump's travel bans have also impacted these companies, with cancellations of a

---

[47] Kenneth Katzman and Christopher M Blanchard, 'Qatar and its Neighbors: Disputes and Possible Implications', CRS Insight, 26 June 2017, p. 3.
[48] The White House, 'Readout of President Donald J. Trump's Call with Amir Sheikh Tameem Bin Hamad Al Thani of Qatar', 7 June 2017.
[49] Katzman and Blanchard, 'Qatar and its Neighbors'.
[50] Tanya Powley and Simeon Kerr, 'A Hard Landing for the Gulf's Airlines', *Financial Times*, 5 September 2017.

significant number of flights to the US. This occurs as US airlines have complained for years that these Gulf companies were unfairly conquering the global market of air travel thanks to their large government subsidies. Delta Air Lines went as far as to release a fifteen-minute video detailing this unfair competition and asking the US government to take action.[51]

These elements call for a sober assessment of Gulf–US relations under Trump. The election of the real-estate tycoon surely created momentum for stronger ties, but it did not tackle the biggest issue, which has been undermining the relationship for the last decade: the increased unpredictability of US policy towards the Gulf, and by extension its waning resolve to protect its GCC partners. Certainly, the US remains the most decisive external actor in the peninsula, thanks to its political clout and its military footprint, but from the reconstruction of post-Saddam Iraq to US policy on the Arab uprising, Gulf states have faced significant upsets that have led them to revisit the nature of their dependency on Washington.

Additionally, the US initiative to develop shale gas to decrease its reliance on imported oil also changed the terms of the economic relationship between the US and the peninsula. By 2035, the US could be producing 342 billion cubic metres of shale gas, which would account for 47 per cent of its total gas production (as opposed to 16 per cent in 2009). In 2013, the International Energy Agency went as far as to predict that the US might become a net energy exporter by 2025, overtaking both Russia as the largest gas producer and Saudi Arabia as the largest oil producer.[52] In light of these developments, Gulf states started looking for other countries to diversify first their trade relations, but soon their strategic partnerships as well.

---

[51] Aviation24 dot be, 'Delta Air Lines Releases Video to Educate Employees on Gulf Carrier Subsidies', YouTube, 3 July 2017, <https://www.youtube.com/watch?v=55HSxI-HlcE>, accessed 13 April 2018.

[52] Jeppe Kofod, 'The Economic and Strategic Implications of the Unconventional Oil and Gas Revolution', General Report for the NATO Parliamentary Assembly Economics and Security Committee, 065 ESC 13 E, 11 March 2013, pp. 2–3.

II. THE RISE OF GULF–ASIAN COMMON STRATEGIC INTERESTS

While the relationship between the GCC and Western countries began to decrease economically and politically, the region increasingly attracted energy-hungry Asian powers – primarily China, India, Japan and South Korea – looking for oil and gas resources required to sustain their growth. Researchers have acknowledged this shift of energy markets towards Asian economies, but so far have tended to downplay its political meaning by focusing on its purely economic logic and modest strategic dimension.[1]

Two legitimate arguments are highlighted in the scholarship. First, as the previous chapter underlined, in the near future the network of US military bases in the Gulf is unlikely to be dismantled, and defence agreements with Washington will continue to shape the security policies of GCC members. Second, Asian countries appear reluctant to develop a geopolitical posture far from their territories. Although strategic thinkers in Washington continue to support the political gain of US global commitments, there is no such ambition in India or China. The former remains trapped in its local conflict with Pakistan and seems unable to project power at the global level, while the latter insisted until recently on the purely economic nature of its diplomacy – the so-called 'China's peaceful rise' – to tone down speculation of Chinese hegemonic aspirations.[2] Because of their inability or their unwillingness to play a global role, those countries were therefore portrayed as 'free riders',

---

[1] For the most comprehensive scholarship on current Gulf–Asia relations, see Christopher Davidson, *The Persian Gulf and Pacific Asia: From Indifference to Interdependence* (London: Hurst, 2010); Geoffrey Kemp, *The East Moves West: India, China, and Asia's Growing Presence in the Middle East* (Washington, DC: Brookings Institution Press, 2010).
[2] Amrita Narlikar, 'Is India a Responsible Great Power?', *Third World Quarterly* (Vol. 32, No. 9, 2011); Degang Sun and Yahia H Zoubir, 'China's Economic Diplomacy Towards the Arab Countries: Challenges Ahead?', *Journal of Contemporary China* (Vol. 24, No. 95, 2015).

importing Gulf oil while enjoying the stable security environment provided by the US military presence in the region.

However, this means that with the rapid changes in the global distribution of wealth, the international politics of the Gulf no longer reflect its international economics. The US may remain the central actor of security policies in the region, but its economy is less dependent on the peninsula than those of China or India. Furthermore, although a decade ago Gulf trade to non-Western countries was quasi-exclusively driven by oil and gas supplies, it now encompasses projects that transcend energy trade. Gulf countries partner with Asian nations in a wide variety of sectors, including high-technology programmes, educational partnerships and mutual investments. These investments touch upon sectors involving national security affairs such as nuclear energy, military platforms and construction of economic corridors that could define the future flow of goods between the regions over the next decades. The large number of flows spanning many areas and the magnitude of investment in each of these have created a web of closely connected issues affecting Gulf–Asian relations, a density of unprecedented breadth that broadens the scope of interregional exchanges. These trends build a new dynamic for Gulf–Asian relations that eventually includes a strong political dimension. Therefore, this paper argues that economic interdependence can lead to a set of common security interests. These ties have direct or indirect effects that can be observed in other fields, specifically the security domain.[3] In this context, this chapter retraces the evolution of Gulf–Asian economics to evidence its growing political dimension. Following an analysis of the evolving energy market, the chapter looks at the development of strategic investments, the emergence of common security interests and the implementation of this rapprochement at the diplomatic level.

The Implications of Evolving Gulf Energy Markets

For leaders in the Arabian Peninsula, energy policies in the Gulf are the primary national security policies. This is a consequence of the well-known rentier model of Gulf economies.[4] Because public budgets in countries such as Saudi Arabia, Kuwait and the UAE still rely primarily on revenue from energy sales, any significant trend in that domain is likely to transcend the economic stakes and impact the whole region at

---

[3] On the idea of fungibility in international relations, see Robert J Art, 'American Foreign Policy and the Fungibility of Force', *Security Studies* (Vol. 5, No. 4, 1996).
[4] In political science and international relations theory, a rentier state is one that derives all or a substantial portion of its national revenues from the rent of indigenous resources to external clients.

Figure 2: China's Crude Oil Imports by Country of Origin, 2014

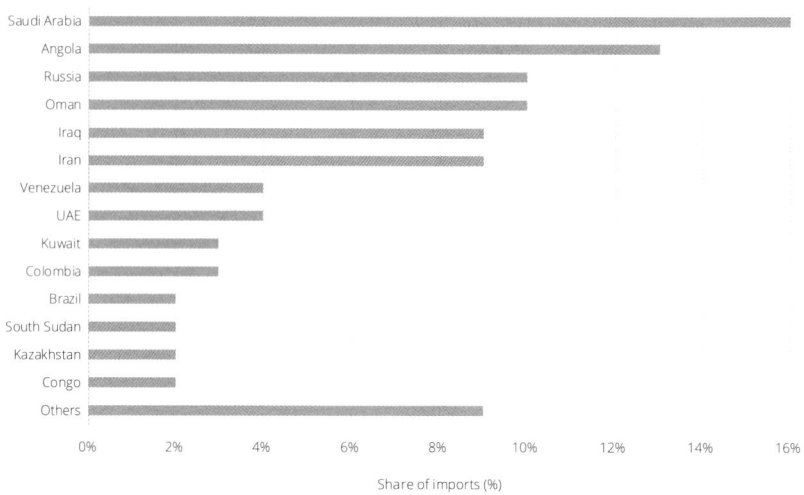

Source: US Energy Information Administration, 'China', International Energy Data and Analysis, last updated 14 May 2015.

the political level.[5] In other words, major changes in Gulf international relations are first the result of the evolving energy markets.

Historically, Gulf countries looked westward for the development of their oil and gas industries.[6] It was Western engineers who enabled local companies such as Saudi Aramco and Abu Dhabi National Oil Company to exploit their resources. Joint ventures with Chevron, British Petroleum, Shell and Total defined the distribution of barrels and it was Gulf energy that fuelled the growth of European and American economies after the Second World War.

Over the last decade, the market has changed as a result of the transformation of the world economy. The share of global wealth of Asian countries increased: according to the IMF, the Asia-Pacific region was estimated to account for 63.3 per cent of global growth in 2017.[7] Continuing population growth and industrial development has accompanied Asian growth. Together, these have generated high levels of

---

[5] On the enduring rentier nature of Gulf economies, see IMF, 'Economic Diversification in Oil-Exporting Arab Countries', April 2016, p. 8.
[6] Jill Crystal, *Oil and Politics in the Gulf: Rulers and Merchants in Kuwait and Qatar* (Cambridge: Cambridge University Press, 1995); Palmer, *Guardians of the Gulf*; Lawrence G Potter (ed.), *The Persian Gulf in History* (New York, NY: Springer, 2009).
[7] IMF, *Asia and Pacific: Preparing for Choppy Seas*, World Economic and Financial Surveys (Washington, DC: IMF, 2017), p. xiii; Enda Curran and Ye Xie, 'Asia Will Hold Global Growth Crown for Next Decade at Least: Q&A', *Bloomberg*, 13 October 2017.

Figure 3: India's Crude Oil Imports by Country of Origin, 2015

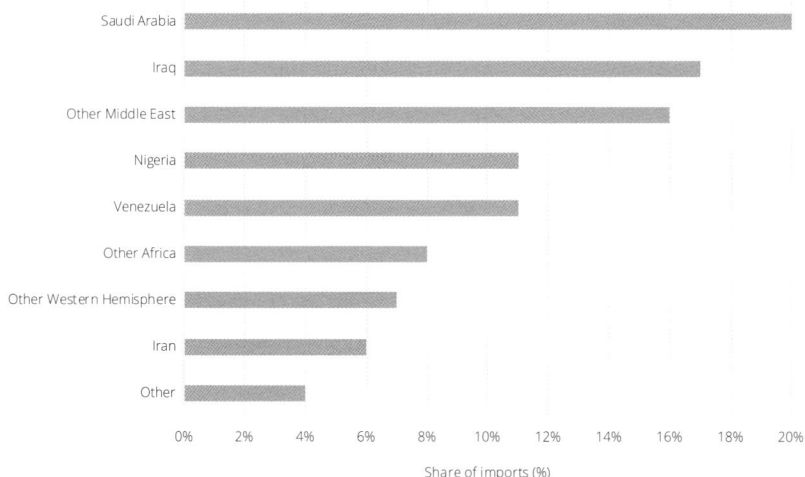

Source: US Energy Information Administration, 'Country Analysis Brief: India', last updated 14 June 2016.

energy demands. Excluding the US, the four biggest importers of oil in the world today are in Asia: China; India; Japan; and South Korea, which together total 40.6 per cent of oil purchases in 2016.[8] This trend is here to stay: over the next fifteen years, the bloc combining China, India and the members of ASEAN will define the consumption of global energy, leaving OECD countries far behind.[9]

In Asia, the primary driver of this rebalancing is China. In 2017, the country was the world's largest growth market for energy for sixteen consecutive years.[10] Saudi Arabia, which accounted for 16 per cent of China's crude oil imports in 2016, is one of its top three providers. When combined with the shares of GCC members, they represent roughly 31 per cent of China's crude oil imports. The figures in the field of liquefied natural gas (LNG) are also worth noting: the Emirate of Qatar alone represents a third of China's LNG imports (34 per cent), with the country with the second-largest share, Indonesia, only reaching 12 per cent.[11]

---

[8] Daniel Workman, 'Crude Oil Imports by Country', World's Top Exports, 29 January 2018, <http://www.worldstopexports.com/crude-oil-imports-by-country/>, accessed 13 April 2018.
[9] Institute of Energy Economics Japan, 'Asia/World Energy Outlook 2016: Consideration of 3E's+S Under New Energy Circumstances in the World', October 2016, p. 2.
[10] BP, 'BP Statistical Review of World Energy: June 2017', 66th edition, 2017, p. 2.
[11] US Energy Information Administration (EIA), 'Country Analysis Brief: China', Report, 14 May 2015, p. 14.

India also shapes these interregional trends as it relies heavily on Gulf oil, with Saudi Arabia being its largest source (20 per cent). Meanwhile, Qatar is India's biggest LNG supplier by far (62 per cent).[12]

Likewise, Japan imports most of its energy needs from the Gulf. In the field of LNG, the Tokyo Power Company signed a supply agreement with the UAE in 1977 – a first in the Gulf – and Japan remains the primary destination of Emirati natural gas, with India in second place. Japanese companies also played a significant role in the development of the Qatari natural gas industry.[13] Following the Fukushima nuclear plant disaster in 2011, Qatar–Japan energy trade grew even more: the accident triggered a shift in the Japanese government's views on energy sources, but in practice, replacing nuclear energy meant Tokyo has had to rely more on Gulf imports. This is how Japan became the main consumer of Qatar's gas, as well as how Qatar became the third-largest source of imported oil, after Saudi Arabia and the UAE.

As seen from the Gulf countries, the rise of Asian energy needs completely changed their customer base. A country such as Saudi Arabia, which traditionally sold to Western markets, now exports 69 per cent of its barrels to Asia (in contrast to 18 per cent to the American continent and 10 per cent to Europe).[14] The figures for the UAE are even more spectacular: in 2016, 96 per cent of UAE crude oil exports were shipped to Asia.[15]

This leads to an increased visibility of Asian companies in Gulf capitals. Japanese stakes in onshore and offshore oil concessions of the Emirate of Abu Dhabi have steadily increased. In autumn 2017, the signing of strategic agreements between Abu Dhabi National Oil Company and Japan's Ministry of Economy, Trade and Industry reflected the growth of the relationship.[16] Meanwhile, in 2011 South Korea won its first energy deals with Abu Dhabi, giving the rights to the state-owned Korea National Oil Corporation for the exploitation of oilfields – representing more than 1 billion barrels.[17] Given the current projections on long-term energy needs in Asia, both Gulf and Asian countries are likely to intensify their ties in this field. On the one hand, this means that Gulf economies – and by extension the stability of the local regimes – will

---

[12] US EIA, 'Country Analysis Brief: India', Report, 14 June 2016, p. 17.
[13] Kohei Hashimoto, Jareer Elass and Stacy Eller, 'Liquefied Natural Gas from Qatar: The Qatargas Project', James A Baker III Institute for Public Policy, Working Paper, December 2004.
[14] US EIA, 'Country Analysis Brief: Saudi Arabia', Report, 20 October 2017, p. 8.
[15] US EIA, 'Country Analysis Brief: United Arab Emirates', Report, 21 March 2017, Overview.
[16] *The National*, 'Adnoc Strikes Strategic Agreements with Japan', 8 October 2017.
[17] Tamsin Carlisle, 'South Korea Strikes Deal for Billion Barrels of Oil', *The National*, 14 March 2011.

be increasingly defined by their Asian customer base, while on the other hand, the economic ambitions of Asian powers will remain attainable as long as their access to Gulf energy markets are protected from disruptive elements, such as local wars, terrorism and maritime piracy.

The Development of Strategic Investments Between the Gulf and Asia

Although energy was the trigger of the Gulf–Asian rapprochement, trade relations between these regions have widened in scope during the past ten years. Cases abound where sectors of Gulf economies traditionally controlled by Western consortia are now operated with or by Asian companies. They involve nuclear energy development, the banking system, and real estate. Furthermore, investments in infrastructure have become a cornerstone of the Gulf–Asian relationship. Infrastructure creates economic corridors that connect both regions and ensure the long-term sustainability of the exchanges.

Going beyond the prism of energy, India's relations with the Gulf have also been expanding at a spectacular rate. According to International Trade Centre figures, for 2014–15 Indian trade with the GCC totalled $137.7 billion (it amounted to $5.5 billion in 2001).[18] In the real-estate business, India is the largest foreign investor in Dubai ($3.26 billion in 2017), while remittances sent to India from workers in the Gulf have now reached the annual sum of $35 billion (around 8.5 million Indian workers currently live in the Gulf).[19] Indian investments go across all areas of Gulf economies, including shopping malls, technology and education institutions.

Similarly, the evolution of Japan–Qatar relations reflects the complexity of exchanges between both regions. As mentioned earlier, bilateral cooperation between Tokyo and Doha initially started with the sale of LNG to Japan, but over the years it has grown to include other industrial sectors. An economic agreement was signed in 2006, followed by the creation of a Japan–Qatar Joint Economic Committee. As Qatar launched several projects designed to modernise the small emirate, Japanese companies positioned themselves for competing bids and opened offices in Doha. It is now estimated that around 50 Japanese companies are present in Qatar.[20] Some successes are worth mentioning: Mitsubishi has been awarded major construction contracts in the

---

[18] Robert Anderson, 'India and the GCC – Bound by History', *Gulf Business*, 12 August 2017.
[19] Gayatri Nayak, 'India to be the Top Recipient of Remittances from its Diaspora in 2017', *Economic Times*, 3 October 2017.
[20] Sameh Saeid, 'Japan Keen to Expand Ties with Qatar Beyond Energy', *Qatar Tribune*, 1 March 2017.

preparation of the World Cup in Qatar in 2022. In 2016, a loan from Japanese banks enabled Qatar to purchase French Rafale fighter jets and missiles – worth \$6.8 billion.[21] In the meantime, Japan has opened its doors to a Qatar Science Campus located in Sendai City and a Qatar Sports Park in Shirakawa.[22]

The development of Gulf relations with other Asian countries follows a similar trajectory. Singapore, a city-state located between the Indian and Pacific Oceans, positions itself as a hub for Asia in the field of refined oil products, and has a strong interest in close partnership with Gulf countries. As it does not have its own hydrocarbon reserves, it relies mostly on the Gulf for its oil and gas consumption, as well as for the onward transit to Asian neighbours.

But the Gulf–Singapore relationship has also widened. In 2008, the island signed the GCC-Singapore Free Trade Agreement (FTA) – a significant achievement given the fact that Singapore was the first country outside the Middle East to conclude such an agreement with the GCC. The declaration of Lee Yi Shyan, then Singapore's senior minister of state for trade and industry, that the FTA would 'further enhance Singapore's role as a Gateway City by connecting the two large regions of Asia and the Middle East & North Africa' further evidenced the logic of turning the country into the conduit between those regions.[23]

Since then, Gulf–Singapore relations have steadily grown. By 2017, the UAE and Saudi Arabia were respectively Singapore's first and second largest trading partners in the region. As with Japan, trade includes various domains. The rulers of the Emirate of Dubai used the urban expertise of Singapore to build their own development strategy.[24] Singapore also provided technical assistance in the field of government capacity-building to Oman and Kuwait. Gulf acquisitions in Singapore have also intensified. The UAE-based Al-Futtaim Group acquired Singapore's Robinsons & Company – one of the largest retailers – in 2008, while the Emirate of Fujairah awarded the Singaporean company SembCorp Utilities with a \$2.5-billion contract to build an integrated water desalination and power plant. SABIC (Saudi Basic Industries Corporation), a global manufacturing company, supervises its Asian operations from

---

[21] Pierre Tran, 'Japan-Qatar Ties Help Fund Rafale Order', *Defense News*, 19 March 2016.
[22] Cinzia Miotto and Giorgio Cafiero, 'The Prospects for Japanese-Qatari Relations', *MENASource*, blog of the Atlantic Council, 22 June 2016.
[23] Singapore Ministry of Foreign Affairs, 'Joint Press Statement on the Gulf Cooperation Council-Singapore Free Trade Agreement 1 September 2013', 1 September 2013.
[24] Samer Bagaeen, 'Brand Dubai: The Instant City; or the Instantly Recognizable City', *International Planning Studies* (Vol. 12, No. 2, 2007), pp. 173–97.

Singapore, and Qatar's DIAR acquired a 40 per cent stake – making it the largest shareholder – of Singapore's famous Raffles Hotel in 2009.

Although the Singaporean and Japanese cases reflect the deepening of Gulf–Asian relations, the examples do not touch on sensitive domains, of which the development of nuclear cooperation is an important illustration. The UAE's 2009 decision to award a South Korean consortium, led by Korea Electric Power Corporation (KEPCO), the contract to build its first four nuclear power plants is an example of this trend. The contract is worth around $40 billion.[25] Described as 'the largest mega-project in Korean history' by government officials in Seoul, the deal came as a surprise, if not a shock, to Washington and Paris. French and American competing groups had been assembled, with strong experience in the export of nuclear technology – an experience that KEPCO did not have. Additionally, the diplomatic environment initially seemed to favour a Western bid. France had just opened a naval base in Abu Dhabi and renewed its defence agreement with the UAE for a further 50 years, and the US and the UAE had signed the 123 Agreement for Peaceful Civilian Nuclear Energy Cooperation in January 2009. This agreement, negotiated under the George W Bush administration, enabled the UAE to receive nuclear technology from the US and underlined the trust between both countries, in a major contrast to the regional suspicions over Iran's proliferation programme. This is also why – despite the fact that the US-based firm Westinghouse Electric was part of the group led by KEPCO – the final choice made in Abu Dhabi came as a major surprise. It indicated both the ability of Asian groups to challenge the primacy that the West has traditionally had in certain fields and the new level of trust reached between Seoul and Abu Dhabi.[26] Planned to start operating in 2020, the four nuclear reactors will sell electricity to the Abu Dhabi Water and Electricity Authority. The plant site is located in Barakah, in the western region of Abu Dhabi near its border with Saudi Arabia. In 2010, a further step was reached when KEPCO purchased shares in the Emirates Nuclear Energy Cooperation, which will eventually operate the plants.[27] Moreover, the contract awarded to KEPCO was not an isolated act. It heralded a steady rapprochement between Abu Dhabi and Seoul across all domains,

---

[25] Amena Bakr and Cho Mee-young, 'South Korea Wins Landmark Gulf Nuclear Power Deal', *Reuters*, 27 December 2009.

[26] Joachim Kolb, 'Small is Beautiful: South Korean-Gulf Relations as an Example of Strategic Engagement by Players in Different Arenas', in Tim Niblock and Monica Malik (eds), *Asia-Gulf Economic Relations in the 21st Century: The Local to Global Transformation* (Berlin: Gerlach Press, 2013).

[27] Christopher M Blanchard and Paul K Kerr, 'The United Arab Emirates Nuclear Program and Proposed U.S. Nuclear Cooperation', Congressional Research Service Report, R40344, 2010, p. 2.

as evidenced by the 2011 contract awarded to Korea National Oil Corporation for the exploitation of Abu Dhabi's oilfields.

Nuclear energy is also becoming a field of cooperation between China and Saudi Arabia, although at a much slower pace. Since declaring its goal to construct nuclear power reactors in 2009 to diversify its energy mix, the Saudi programme has been modestly progressing. Still, a memorandum of understanding (MoU) between China and Saudi Arabia was signed in January 2012 aimed at strengthening bilateral scientific and economic exchanges. In particular, China is to develop nuclear power plants and research plants for the kingdom.

It is worth mentioning that Riyadh has also signed similar agreements with other countries, such as France, Russia and the US, and South Korea's Atomic Energy Research Institute was mandated in March 2015 to provide an engineering study on the building of Saudi Arabia's nuclear reactors. Nonetheless, the nuclear issue was on the agenda of King Salman's visit to China in March 2017, which was used to revive the 2012 agreement with a more ambitious cooperation agreement. This bilateral initiative now involves joint projects between China National Nuclear Corporation and the Saudi Geological Survey in the exploration of fissile materials, and between King Abdullah City for Atomic and Renewable Energy and China Nuclear Engineering Group Corporation in the development of water desalination with the use of gas-cooled nuclear reactors.[28] Given the limited outcomes of this bilateral cooperation so far, it remains to be seen if nuclear energy can seriously become a pillar of Saudi–Chinese relations.

It is in the field of infrastructure that investments between the Gulf and Asia have played the most important role in raising the relationship to a political level. Indeed, Gulf states have quickly understood the benefits of investing in Asian infrastructures through their sovereign wealth funds to secure long-term exports of their energy supplies. At the same time, Gulf infrastructure investments in Asia are an indirect illustration of India–China competition in the building of regional economic networks.

Indeed, the UAE–India rapprochement in recent years included significant Emirati investments in Indian infrastructure. In 2016, Indian Prime Minister Narendra Modi's government launched a ten-year plan of national urban development costing $1.5 trillion,[29] in which Emirati investments play a critical part: a joint investment fund has been created by Delhi and Abu Dhabi with the aim of financing projects worth $75

---

[28] *Reuters*, 'Saudi Arabia Signs Cooperation Deals with China on Nuclear Energy', 25 August 2017.
[29] *Times of India*, 'India Needs $1.5 Trillion for Infrastructure, Arun Jaitley Says', 26 June 2016.

billion – 5 per cent of the total estimated costs.[30] However, the operation of this Indian–Emirati cooperation plan remains unclear. In February 2016, Dubai ports operator DP World announced its intention to invest $1 billion in India-based terminals. However, for most of the remainder of the required investment, observers have been left in the dark. The governance of the investment fund has been a contentious issue and reflects, more broadly, the limits of Modi's ability to modernise India's bureaucracy.[31]

This is in contrast to the more advanced Chinese infrastructure projects. Although Indian–Gulf relations have the potential to grow, GCC rulers do not intend to do so at the cost of their cooperation with China. This is clear from the way GCC countries intend to position themselves as pivotal actors in China's new energy policy summarised by the much-discussed Belt and Road Initiative (BRI).[32]

As a key driver of the foreign policy agenda of President Xi Jinping, the project aims to connect ground and sea supply lines between Europe and China. Using a lyrical analogy, Chinese Foreign Minister Wang Yi described the BRI as 'a symphony performed by all relevant countries'.[33] It involves not only diplomatic talks with European, African and Asian partners, but also major industrial projects. In May 2017, Beijing convened the Silk Road summit for international cooperation that served as a platform to promote the BRI, during which Xi announced a Chinese fund of $124 billion to support contributing countries through various grants and loans.

Noticeably, Gulf countries seem, so far, to be absent from China's grand strategy. In fact, two of the six infrastructure projects in the BRI – the China–Pakistan Economic Corridor and the China–Central Asia–West Asia Economic Corridor – simply bypass the region. At sea, the Chinese route connects Europe to its mainland by crossing the Red Sea and then passing through the Indian Ocean. On land, the BRI goes from Turkey to Central Asia through Iran. The Pakistani port of Gwadar would also operate as an entry point from the Indian Ocean to transit goods to China.[34]

---

[30] Indrani Bagchi, 'India, UAE Push Investment Bond', *Times of India*, 26 February 2017.
[31] Archis Mohan, 'UAE Says Ball in India's Court to Set up $75 Billion Investment Fund', *Business Standard*, 24 January 2017.
[32] Jonathan Fulton, 'The G.C.C. Countries and China's Belt and Road Initiative (BRI): Curbing Their Enthusiasm?', Middle East Institute, 17 October 2017.
[33] *Xinhua*, 'China's Belt and Road Initiatives Not Solo, but Symphony', *China Daily*, 8 March 2015.
[34] See map and details in Peter Cai, 'Understanding China's Belt and Road Initiative', Lowy Institute Analysis, March 2017, p. 2.

Concerned that the implementation of the BRI may sideline the Arabian Peninsula – the fact that Iran plays a major role in the China–Central Asia–West Asia Economic Corridor further increases these concerns – Gulf leaders have been active in promoting their potential role to China. In particular, Saudi Arabia emphasised its key position on the Red Sea and the Gulf of Aden. Interestingly, the rulers in Riyadh adapted their rhetoric to connect the BRI to their own plan of reforms, known as Vision 2030. While visiting Beijing in August 2016, Crown Prince Mohammad bin Salman portrayed the BRI as 'one of the main pillars of the Saudi Vision 2030 which would seek to make China among the kingdom's biggest economic partners'.[35] In light of this, Saudi Arabia has designed a strategy of reciprocal investments: Aramco Asia would expand its support to the development of the Chinese provinces of Fujian and Yunnan in return for Chinese investment in Jazan Economic City on the southern Red Sea coast.[36] Following the UAE model of modernisation, this Saudi development strategy aims to turn this Red Sea area into a future trade hub linking Europe, Africa and Asia, and will determine the ability of the kingdom to position itself as a major regional actor of the BRI.[37]

In other cases, Gulf states have emphasised their ability – contrary to most of the countries involved in the BRI – to finance major infrastructure programmes. It is worth noting that China's Asian Infrastructure and Investment Bank (AIIB) is likely to become a major actor of BRI investments and that five of the GCC countries – Saudi Arabia, Qatar, Kuwait, the UAE and Oman – happen to be members.

Moreover, Gulf officials have underlined the fact that their infrastructures are already robust and could easily serve the Chinese global strategy, a view that the Emirates of Abu Dhabi and Dubai have been actively promoting. For instance, the chief executive of Abu Dhabi Ports, Mohamed Juma Al-Shamisi, has publicly made the case for the country's participation in China's BRI. In a media interview, he described the bilateral relationship between the UAE and China as 'strong' and bringing a 'momentum' for future cooperation in the context of the BRI. His argument is driven by the state of UAE ports in the region. Although Dubai Ports World is already a major player in maritime trade, Abu Dhabi's Khalifa Port is in the process of doubling its capacity in container transportation, a move that aims to put the city at the forefront of the

---

[35]   Mohammad bin Salman quoted in *Arab News*, 'Fusing Vision 2030 with Belt Road Initiative', 3 September 2016.
[36]   Martin Menachery, 'Aramco Asia Develops Synergy Between Saudi Vision 2030, "Belt & Road" Initiative', *Arabian Oil and Gas*, 6 September 2017.
[37]   Naser Al-Tamimi, 'KSA's Important Role in the Chinese Belt and Road Initiative', *Arab News*, 13 May 2017.

shipping industry linking the Gulf to Asia.[38] Additionally, the port in Fujairah, the eastern emirate of the UAE with a coastline on the Gulf of Oman, has also increased the number of its berths and its storage capacity, with the long-term aim of competing with the world-class ports of Rotterdam and Singapore.[39] Given the fact that approximately 60 per cent of Chinese–Emirati trade is re-exported to African and European final destinations, it makes sense to consider the local ports as regional nodes for the BRI.[40]

However, it is in neither the UAE nor in Saudi Arabia that China has so far decided to look for a Gulf point of access, but in the Sultanate of Oman. In 2016 both countries signed an agreement allowing a Chinese consortium to build an industrial city in Duqm, a growth town on the coast of the Arabian Sea. The project is worth $10.7 billion and, if completed, could turn the area into a major hub on the Indian Ocean.[41]

Given the fact that some of the Chinese projects are still in their infancy, changes may still occur, especially since numerous political and financial uncertainties surrounding the BRI remain. But overall, the Gulf region's strategy regarding the BRI is the latest illustration of Gulf–Asian exchanges showing a new complexity of relations between both regions, and according to economic projections, the strength of these ties is unlikely to decrease. These reciprocal investments consolidate the relationship that energy trade initiated, framing the bilateral relations and eventually implying the emergence of common security interests.

The Emergence of Common Security Interests

This emphasis on infrastructure investment reflects a core priority for both sides (supply and demand): ensuring the uninterrupted flow of commodities necessary for Gulf and Asian economies. By extension, this means a shared interest in supporting regional political stability. In other words, the growing economic ties between Gulf and Asian countries trigger inter-regional security interests. In some ways, this does not differ from the origins of Western interests in the Gulf. Historically, the British Empire primarily involved itself in Gulf local politics – establishing the Trucial States in 1820, emirates that were British protectorates until 1971

---

[38] Mohamed Juma Al Shamisi, 'UAE to Benefit from China's One Belt, One Road Programme', *The National*, 29 July 2017.

[39] Binsal Abdul Kader, 'UAE Stands with Developed Countries in Maritime Field', *Gulf News*, 27 November 2017.

[40] Giorgio Cafiero and Daniel Wagner, 'What the Gulf States Think of "One Belt, One Road"', *The Diplomat*, 24 May 2017.

[41] Wade Shepard, 'Why China is Building a New City Out in the Desert of Oman', *Forbes*, 8 September 2017.

and subsequently formed the UAE – because the peninsula was a key transitory point on the road to British India. The British strategy – and later the American one – was therefore guided by the need for stability, which meant preserving the existing status quo among local players and preventing hegemonic aspirations (in particular those of Iran and Iraq).

However, the emerging security interests between the Gulf and Asian countries also differ from the relations Arab monarchies built with Western powers in some important ways. The absence of a colonial legacy between Gulf and Asian states puts aside misperceptions and prejudices that very frequently shape Arab–Western interactions. More importantly, leaders of the Gulf regimes tend to appreciate Asian reluctance to interfere in regional and local affairs in the way the US and European countries do. They might disagree on specific policies, but there is a common understanding that ensuring regional stability without inciting internal political change serves their mutual interests. Furthermore, in a country such as China, rulers do not face the domestic constraints of Western leaders in justifying their policies with Gulf regimes to their constituencies.

When comparing the political systems in the Gulf and Asia, this convergence is by no means a natural outcome. The Chinese and Saudi political systems, for example, differ widely in their ideologies and structures – a communist bureaucracy versus a religious-based monarchy – but they share a common belief at a global level in maintaining the status quo and preventing interference in the domestic policies of another country. This is explicitly mentioned in the first paragraph of China's Arab Policy Paper, issued in 2016.[42] The first document to state China's strategy towards the Arab World, it acknowledges the convergence with Arab regimes on 'safeguarding state sovereignty and territorial integrity, defending national dignity, seeking political resolution to hotspot issues, and promoting peace and stability in the Middle East'.[43]

The rhetoric of human rights and democratic reforms that Western leaders frequently use in their foreign policy speeches is absent from those of Chinese and Gulf rulers. This explains how China consistently refrained from commenting on Gulf internal affairs, while GCC members have kept their distance from issues such as the status of Taiwan or even the treatment of the Muslim Uighur community in China. The absence of ideological positions in Gulf–Chinese relations contrasts with the more complicated framework of US–Gulf relations.

---

[42] People's Republic of China, 'China's Arab Policy Paper', *Xinhua*, January 2016, <http://news.xinhuanet.com/english/china/2016-01/13/c_135006619.htm>, accessed 13 April 2018.
[43] *Ibid.*

Notably, Wu Bingbing, an associate professor at Peking University, writes that China's policy in the Gulf is driven by four geopolitical objectives: 'to refuse any single power's unilateral control of the whole region, to prevent the emergence of any anti-Chinese regime in the region, to oppose any formal support of Taiwanese independence forces or other separatist forces in China by Gulf countries' governments, and to pursue possible and potential support from the Gulf region for China's foreign strategy'.[44] In other words, China's goal in its engagement in the region is to consolidate the existing status quo while expecting a similar attitude from Gulf leaders towards the Asia-Pacific region.

A similar approach can be applied to Russia–GCC relations. Gulf leaders may disagree with some of President Vladimir Putin's assertive policies – in particular on the Russian military intervention in Syria – but they tend to appreciate his strongman leadership style.[45] Russia's diplomatic discourse on preventing regime change interventions in the name of democracy and its emphasis on fighting Islamic extremism as a national security priority echo the concerns of the Gulf rulers, in particular in Saudi Arabia and the UAE.[46]

In this context, Asian and Gulf decision-makers are similarly anxious about the scenarios of insecurity that could disrupt the flow of their trade relations, which could take multiple forms. It may be a local conflict escalating horizontally: for instance, a confrontation between the GCC and Iran, or between India and Pakistan, or even India and China, which triggers a maritime spillover affecting the sea-lanes in the Indian Ocean. Likewise, security vacuums and state failure – the protracted collapse of Yemen being a case in point – can generate a number of non-state threats (piracy, terrorism, organised crime) that also compromise the circulation of goods between the Gulf and Asia.

Piracy provides a good example of this convergence of views. Starting in 2008, the participation of Gulf and Asian navies in counterpiracy operations in the Indian Ocean, and more particularly in the Gulf of Aden, has indicated a common interest in preventing the disruption of maritime

---

[44] Wu Bingbing, 'Strategy and Politics in the Gulf as Seen from China', in Bryce Wakefield and Susan L Levenstein (eds), *China and the Persian Gulf: Implications for the United States* (Washington, DC: Woodrow Wilson International Center for Scholars, 2011), p. 10.

[45] Paul Stronski and Richard Sokolsky, 'The Return of Global Russia: An Analytical Framework', Carnegie Endowment for International Peace, 14 December 2017; Stephen Blank, 'The Foundations of Russian Policy in the Middle East', Jamestown Foundation, 5 October 2017; Leone Lakhani, 'Russia-Gulf Arab States: A Relationship of Convenience', *Cipher Brief*, 7 March 2017.

[46] Samuel Ramani, 'How Russia is Courting the Gulf', *National Interest*, 1 August 2016; Lakhani, 'Russia-Gulf Arab States'.

trade caused by a surge in attacks – an increase of more than 60 per cent between 2007 and 2008 according to the International Maritime Bureau – and, moreover, the resolve of these countries to deploy their own military assets to curb the phenomenon.[47] This piracy phenomenon constituted a major threat to both Gulf and Asian countries. Attacks targeted merchant vessels, meaning possible shortages and a significant increase in insurance costs. By March 2011, UAE's Minister for Foreign Affairs Sheikh Abdullah bin Zayed Al-Nahyan described piracy as 'one of the most threatening challenges of the 21st century'.[48]

For China, the decision to send three warships (including two of its most advanced destroyers) in December 2008 to the Gulf of Aden was a major turn in its maritime policy. Historians have estimated that the last similar maritime expedition into the Indian Ocean was in the 1400s.[49] Likewise, South Korea approved the first foreign deployment of its naval forces – including one destroyer, a crew of 300 personnel and a helicopter – to join the US-led Combined Task Force 151 (CTF-151) in the Gulf of Aden, three months after the Chinese precedent.[50] South Korea later took command of the CTF-151, whose headquarters are located in Bahrain with the US Navy Fifth Fleet. Gulf countries such as Saudi Arabia, Oman, Qatar and the UAE also contributed, though rather modestly, to the CTF-151. In the meantime, Saudi Arabia, Japan, India and Iran also conducted their own maritime operations.[51]

Interestingly, the piracy phenomenon in the Gulf of Aden marked a departure for both Gulf and Asian navies. It revived national ambitions to build maritime forces able to project forces far from their shores. Two years later, the commander of the UAE Navy, Brigadier Ibrahim Al-Musharrakh, called for GCC leadership over the security of the Gulf waterways, an assertion far from the previous passivity of local actors. This was followed by the GCC initiative to build a maritime coordination

---

[47] Rick 'Ozzie' Nelson and Scott Goossens, 'Counter-Piracy in the Arabian Sea: Challenges and Opportunities for GCC Action', Gulf Analysis Paper, Center for Strategic and International Studies, May 2011, p. 2.
[48] Abdullah bin Zayed Al-Nahyan quoted in *Emirates News Agency*, 'Maritime Piracy is Quickly Becoming One of the Most Threatening Challenges of 21st Century: Abdullah', 2 March 2011.
[49] Andrew S Erickson and Justin D Mikolay, 'Welcome China to the Fight Against Pirates', *Proceedings* (Vol. 135, No. 3, March 2009).
[50] On the history of South Korea's contribution to the counterpiracy operations, see Terence Roehrig, 'South Korea's Counterpiracy Operations in the Gulf of Aden', in Scott A Snyder et al. (eds), *Global Korea: South Korea's Contributions to International Security* (New York, NY: Council on Foreign Relations Press, 2012), pp. 28–44.
[51] Loveday Morris, 'A Regional Solution to Gulf Naval Security', *The National*, 18 April 2010.

cell in Bahrain to strengthen regional cooperation among national navies. Likewise, the counterpiracy operations paved the way for the regional expansion of Asian navies. This was evidenced by the ambitious procurement policies of these countries and by new overseas basing arrangements.[52] In 2011, Japan inaugurated its first naval base abroad since the Second World War in Djibouti. Five years later, Djibouti also approved the construction of a Chinese base.

In addition to the piracy phenomenon, violent extremist organisations are another topic of common concern for Gulf and Asian countries. In particular, the development of local branches of Daesh (also known as the Islamic State of Iraq and Syria, ISIS) in Southeast Asia brought counterterrorism as a new item on the agenda of bilateral exchanges. It is no surprise that the visit of King Salman to Malaysia – as part of his multi-nation tour of Asia – led the two countries to announce the setting up of the King Salman Centre for International Peace, which will operate as a platform for the armed forces of both countries to share experiences in the counterterrorism domain.[53]

The issue of counterterrorism may coincide with the rise of economic ties between both regions, but there is no chain of causation. It relates, more historically, to the cultural and religious exchanges between the Gulf and Asia.[54] Islamic terrorism is not a new phenomenon in Asia. In South Asia, these organisations have played a central role in the India–Pakistan conflict – in particular in the Kashmir region – for decades. In Southeast Asia, Al-Qa'ida-affiliated groups were responsible for several attacks, such as the 2002 Bali bombings and the 2003 Marriott Hotel bombing in Jakarta. Although counterterrorism policies were subsequently adapted, the resurgence of these attacks in 2016 in the Philippines and Indonesia indicated a new era marked by the influence of Daesh, which translated into pledges of allegiance by local radical organisations. Between 700 and 800 Southeast Asian jihadists left for Syria and Iraq, the majority of them from Indonesia, followed by Malaysia, Singapore and the Philippines. This trend should obviously not be overstated as the numbers are much smaller than those of European nations.[55] Moreover, the link between

---

[52] Geoffrey Till, *Asia's Naval Expansion: An Arms Race in the Making?*, Adelphi Papers 432–433 (London: Routledge, 2012).

[53] Habib Toumi, 'Saudi Arabia, Malaysia Establish Centre for Peace', *Gulf News*, 1 March 2017.

[54] Fred von der Mehden, *Two Worlds of Islam: Interaction Between Southeast Asia and the Middle East* (Gainesville, FA: University Press of Florida, 1993); Angel Rabasa, *Political Islam in Southeast Asia: Moderates, Radicals and Terrorists* (London: Routledge, 2014).

[55] Edward Delman, 'ISIS in the World's Largest Muslim Country: Why are so Few Indonesians Joining the Islamic State?', *The Atlantic*, 3 January 2016.

Daesh in the Middle East and the Gulf and Daesh's local Asian branches should also not be exaggerated: although there have been exchanges and public allegiances, Daesh's global operations do not follow a tight top-down structure. Local leaderships and agendas prevail and the relation to the group in Syria and Iraq is loosely sustained. Still, Gulf and Southeast Asian countries share a common interest in preventing the growth of Islamic militancy. This leads countries from both regions to share counterterrorism experiences and to discuss enhancing the responsible role of Gulf charitable organisations – major donors of aid to Muslim communities in Southeast Asia – to prevent radicalism.[56]

The mix of economic interdependence and common threats – whether from piracy or terrorist organisations – progressively shapes the framework of Gulf–Asian relations. Because political stability is required to guarantee the burgeoning economic relationship, the argument of an exclusively business-driven dialogue is no longer valid. It may not demand an alternative to the pre-existing security arrangements with Western partners, but it undoubtedly calls for exchanges. This is why the past decade has been a period marked by an unprecedented intensification of the diplomatic relations between the regions.

The Gulf–Asia Diplomatic Momentum in the Shadow of China–India Competition

The past few years have witnessed an impressive inflation of diplomatic meetings between Gulf and Asian officials, in particular from China and India. Although Japan and South Korea are cultivating their political exchanges with the GCC, it is mainly the two biggest Asian powers that have brought about the current diplomatic momentum. To understand its significance, it should be compared with the past practices of embassies and ministries of foreign affairs in both regions. While Asian diplomatic representatives have been working in the GCC for a long time, their activity has usually been reduced to consular and trade affairs, and because the Western powers monopolised the security domain, strategic matters were barely on the agenda. Moreover, the Cold War framework prevented significant exchanges between Arab monarchies, which were closely aligned with the US, and communist China, and India, a non-aligned country which relied on the USSR for arms sales and military cooperation.

---

[56] Hilman Latief, 'Gulf Charitable Organizations in Southeast Asia', Middle East Institute, 24 December 2014.

In this context, the establishment of diplomatic relations between Gulf countries and the People's Republic of China (PRC) was remarkably slow and mostly dictated by the American engagement with Beijing under President Richard Nixon. Kuwait first initiated these exchanges in 1971, and was followed by Oman (1978), UAE (1984), Qatar (1988) and Bahrain (1989). It was only in 1990 that Saudi Arabia formally opened diplomatic relations with the PRC, although both countries had significant exchanges prior to that date, as evidenced by the controversial Chinese sale of CSS-2 intermediate-range ballistic missiles to Saudi Arabia in the 1980s.[57] Gulf relations with India were formally less complicated, but no more active than those with China. In addition to the Cold War matrix which put the Gulf states and India into opposing camps, the Gulf–Pakistani military relationship (discussed further in Chapter IV) further impeded the development of ties with Delhi.

The end of the Cold War may have removed a structural obstacle, but it was only in the 2000s, mostly because of the new economic environment, that the political exchanges grew in earnest. This new diplomatic momentum emerged in parallel between Gulf states and India and China. In practice, it meant an increase in the number of high-level visits – heads of state, ministers of foreign affairs and defence – which were followed by the signature of political agreements to build a new framework for these relations which would include regular consultations. This rapprochement indicated, therefore, the intention of GCC leaders to give some weight to the speculation over their new relations with Asian partners.

With regard to the Gulf–China relationship, the diplomatic momentum in the mid-2000s was linked to China's increased reliance on energy imports from the peninsula mentioned earlier, and the simultaneous rhetoric on China's 'peaceful rise' by its leaders. The discourse defused foreign fears of a Chinese hegemonic aspiration while allowing Beijing to gradually raise its global ambitions.[58] Revealingly, after assuming the throne of Saudi Arabia in 2006, King Abdullah chose China as his first visit to a foreign country, during which five agreements on energy cooperation were signed. In a rather lyrical address to welcome the Saudi monarch, then President Hu Jintao declared that the trip 'will write a new chapter of friendly cooperation between China and Saudi Arabia in the new century'.[59] President Hu reciprocated with two visits to Riyadh in the following three

---

[57] Kemp, *The East Moves West*, p. 80.

[58] Jianyong Yue, 'Peaceful Rise of China: Myth or Reality?', *International Politics* (Vol. 45, No. 4, July 2008); Zheng Bijian, 'China's "Peaceful Rise" to Great-Power Status', *Foreign Affairs* (Vol. 84, No. 5, 2005).

[59] Hu Jintao quoted in *Taipei Times*, 'China and Saudi Arabia Sign Historic Energy Deal', 24 January 2006.

years,[60] and a similar pattern followed in the rest of the Gulf, with GCC heads of state visiting Beijing.[61] In addition to the revival of bilateral relations, China also created a multilateral framework through the establishment of a China–GCC Strategic Dialogue, whose first round was held in June 2010 in Beijing. The meeting concluded with the signing of an MoU on strategic dialogue. An action plan for cooperation was later developed in 2014.[62] Chinese and Gulf foreign ministers have so far convened three times for this Strategic Dialogue and China's 2016 Arab Policy Paper explicitly depicted the GCC as one of its primary diplomatic interlocutors in the region.[63]

Like China, India launched its own Gulf policy in the mid-2000s. Given the Cold War environment and traditional Gulf–Pakistan ties, India had barely taken into consideration the strategic dimension of its relations with the Gulf Arab states and historically favoured ties with Iraq and Iran. However, by the end of the 1990s, countries such as the UAE and Saudi Arabia had become such important business partners for Indian companies that the governments in Delhi could no longer ignore the relationship. As a result, in early 2003, the government of then Prime Minister Atal Bihari Vajpayee (from the Bharatiya Janata Party, BJP) announced a programme designed to build India as a global power whose influence would be felt across the Indian Ocean, the Arab Peninsula and the rest of Asia.[64] The same year, a GCC–India political dialogue was initiated. India's new approach towards the Gulf was summarised by the 'Look West' policy, which was officially adopted by the Indian government in 2005. It echoed and complemented the 'Look East' policy, a major effort by Delhi to strengthen its ties with East Asian countries at the economic, political and military level.[65] In the words of Vajpayee's successor, Prime Minister Manmohan Singh, the Gulf region was 'part of our natural economic hinterland'.[66]

---

[60] Daniel Wagner and Theodore Karasik, 'The Maturing Saudi-China Alliance', *Real Clear World*, 7 April 2010.
[61] Neil Quilliam, 'China and the Gulf Co-operation Council: The Rebound Relationship', in Niv Horesh (ed.), *Toward Well-Oiled Relations? China's Presence in the Middle East Following the Arab Spring* (Basingstoke: Palgrave Macmillan, 2016), p. 149.
[62] Mission of the People's Republic of China to the European Union, 'Third Round of China-Gulf Cooperation Council Strategic Dialogue Held in Beijing', Mission of the People's Republic of China to the European Union, press release, 17 January 2014.
[63] People's Republic of China, 'China's Arab Policy Paper'.
[64] Vivek Raghuvanshi, 'India Aims to Project Power Across Asia', *Defense News*, 10 November 2003.
[65] Sanjaya Baru, 'The Sprouting of the "Look West" Policy', *The Hindu*, 19 August 2015.
[66] Government of India, 'PM Launches "Look West" Policy to Boost Cooperation with Gulf', press release, 27 July 2005.

As with China, it is with Saudi Arabia that India first built its new policy in the Gulf, as shown by the visit of King Abdullah to Delhi in January 2006. The Saudi leader signed during this visit the Delhi Declaration, which envisioned a common strategic framework for the bilateral relationship. It was followed four years later by a visit to Saudi Arabia of India's then prime minister, Manmohan Singh, and the signing of the Riyadh Declaration, which stipulated that both countries had 'decided to raise their cooperation to a strategic partnership covering security, economic, defence and political areas', affirming that 'tolerance, religious harmony and brotherhood, irrespective of faith or ethnic background, were part of the principles and values of both countries'.[67] The strategic implications, however, of the new declaration were still vague. Moreover, as is analysed in Chapter IV, the reinforcement of Riyadh's relations with India did not lead to a significant revision of its traditional close partnership with Pakistan, India's arch enemy. When asked informally, officers and diplomats from Saudi Arabia underline the strategic importance of India as 'the next global player', but remain cautious of suggesting that this would affect their older relationship with Pakistan.[68]

Despite the ambitious announcements, Manmohan Singh's Gulf policy proved to be primarily, if not exclusively, a policy towards Saudi Arabia. Following the promotion of the new Saudi–Indian partnership, it was two long years before Singh visited other Gulf countries (Oman and Qatar) where MoUs covering defence, investment and energy matters were signed.[69] India's then Vice-President Mohammad Hamid Ansari visited Kuwait the following year, during which three agreements – in the field of education and scientific cooperation – were signed.

The election of India's Prime Minister Narendra Modi in May 2014 triggered a new dynamic, whereby the most significant rapprochement was not with Saudi Arabia but with the UAE. Although it was formally initiated in 2003, it took a decade to take off. Specifically, in August 2015, Modi travelled to the UAE – the first Indian prime minister to do so since Indira Gandhi in 1981. Modi met with the Emirati authorities as well as with the local Indian community, around 2.6 million (or 30 per cent) of the total population. Approximately 40,000 of them came to the Dubai Cricket Stadium to listen to Modi's speech, which looked like a giant

---

[67] Prime Minister's Office, 'Riyadh Declaration: A New Era of Strategic Partnership', 28 February 2010, <http://pib.nic.in/newsite/erelcontent.aspx?relid=58617>, accessed 17 April 2018.
[68] Author's interviews with representatives of the Royal Saudi Armed Forces, Rome, 13 March 2012.
[69] Prasanta Kumar Pradhan, 'Accelerating India's "Look West Policy" in the Gulf', Institute for Defence Studies and Analyses, IDSA Issue Brief, 3 February 2011, p. 2.

entertainment performance. Crown Prince Mohammed bin Zayed Al-Nahyan of Abu Dhabi, the architect of the new UAE foreign policy, followed Modi's visit to Delhi in January 2016, and other ministerial meetings increased in frequency between the two sides.

Bin Zayed was then invited as the chief guest at India's Republic Day celebrations in January 2017, a gesture that revealed the new proximity between India and Emirati leaders. Bin Zayed and Modi co-authored a manifesto in the UAE-based newspaper *The National*. Describing their rapprochement as driven by a 'common desire to build a resilient modern strategic partnership', they expressed their condemnation of 'terrorism in the name of religious or political objectives', and underlined their joint military activities, economic investment plans and prospects for space cooperation.[70] The manifesto reflected a change in tone and substance. Far removed from the previous statements of the past decade, it read as a confirmation of a rapprochement driven by political motivations at the highest level. Speeches from Emirati and Indian officials were no longer vague statements about a shared culture and broad commitment to peace and cooperation, but rather the expression of a strategic convergence on topics such as counterterrorism and maritime security.

This revival of India's Gulf policy is driven by several interrelated factors. Common interests regarding energy security in the Indian Ocean surely play a role, but the new impetus brought about by Modi is also an indirect consequence of India's degraded relations with China and Pakistan.[71] More specifically, India's Gulf policy under Modi may try to balance the former while containing the incursions of the latter. Given the asymmetry between the Chinese and Indian economies, Delhi fears that the increasing Chinese presence in the Gulf – both economically and diplomatically – could eventually shape the strategic environment in one of its neighbouring areas. In fact, Indian policymakers are already witnessing this reality in East Asia, where Chinese initiatives dwarf their own plans of building partnerships with local countries.[72] In other words, India's active policy in the Gulf – especially as the role of the peninsula in the Chinese BRI is still unclear – could help alleviate the risk of a future encirclement by China.

At the same time, India may be tempted to drive a wedge between the GCC and Pakistan, historically an influential actor in the peninsula, to isolate

---

[70] Sheikh Mohammed bin Zayed and Narendra Modi, 'From our Bond of Personal Friendship, a Bold New Vision', *The National*, 26 January 2017.

[71] See the articles on Narendra Modi in the special issue on India's foreign policy of *International Affairs* (Vol. 93, No. 1, January 2017).

[72] Frédéric Grare, *India Turns East: International Engagement and US–China Rivalry* (London: Hurst, 2017).

the latter diplomatically. The India–Pakistan political dialogue remains in deadlock, and for several years the security approach has been the prevailing one, as reflected by the intensity of Indian retaliatory strikes in September 2016 on a terrorist camp inside Pakistan.[73] India subsequently pressured South Asian countries to cancel the Summit of the South Asian Association for Regional Cooperation (SAARC), which was to take place in Islamabad at the end of 2016.[74] Likewise, Delhi's emphasis on counterterrorism in the Indian–Emirati rapprochement is partly aimed at targeting Pakistan as a factor of instability, not only for India but for Gulf kingdoms as well. In this context, the Pakistani decision not to join the Saudi-led coalition in Yemen in 2015 opened a window of opportunity for Delhi. Although this strategy of isolating Islamabad may not fully achieve its goal, it could constrain the Pakistani leadership, at least in the short term.

More broadly, the Indian–Chinese competition over their relations with Gulf countries shows how much political calculations are now shaping interactions. The inter-regional ties may have been initially triggered by the evolving energy markets, but they quickly expanded because of strategic investment that transcends the mere equation of energy consumption. Eventually, this culminated in the new momentum illustrated by high-level diplomatic visits and multiple bilateral agreements. But assessing the rapprochement cannot be limited to indicators such as economic interdependence and diplomatic meetings, and therefore the next two chapters look at the operation of these relations in terms of security cooperation and their consequences on the geopolitics of both the Gulf and Asia.

---

[73] Nitin A Gokhale, 'The Inside Story of India's 2016 Surgical Strikes', *The Diplomat*, 23 September 2017.
[74] Smruti S Pattanaik, 'Cancellation of the SAARC Summit: Has India Succeeded in Isolating Pakistan Regionally?', Institute for Defence Studies and Analyses, IDSA Comment, 29 September 2016.

III. THE POLITICS OF GULF–ASIAN SECURITY COOPERATION

Security cooperation remains the most concrete expression of a rapprochement between two countries. It indicates the operation of a diplomatic proximity and ensures that public pledges are substantiated. At the same time, bilateral security cooperation can only become effective if the capabilities of both sides are meaningful by themselves. In other words, exchanges between security forces – intelligence services, military or police forces – will have strategic significance not simply because of the aspirations of national leaders, but because of technical criteria: the readiness and interoperability of their personnel; the frequency of their interactions with the other side; and the scope of the exchanges all inform the level of operation for a bilateral security cooperation. This is why, in the case of Gulf–Asian relations, this cooperation has to be understood in the broader context of the evolution of both Asian and Gulf security politics.

During the past decade, while Gulf energy exports have leaned towards the Asia-Pacific region, national armed forces in the peninsula have undergone an ambitious modernisation process.[1] The traditional reliance on US protection through military bases operated by US armed forces in the region remains valid, but its extent has lessened compared to the 1990s. This is the result of changes in terms of capabilities, training and strategic ambitions of Gulf states. The massive arms sales of the past two decades and the rise of a new generation of officers educated since the 1991 Gulf War are now turning the militaries of countries such as Saudi Arabia and the UAE into major regional players.[2] At the same time, Gulf leaders have become more strategically ambitious. The UAE and Qatar contributed to NATO air operations in Libya in 2011 as well as to

---

[1] On the evolution of armed forces in the Gulf, see Anthony Cordesman and Abdullah Toukan, *Iran and the Gulf Military Balance* (Washington, DC: Center for Strategic and International Studies, 2016).

[2] Nadim Hasbani, 'The Geopolitics of Weapons Procurement in the Gulf States', *Defense & Security Analysis* (Vol. 22, No. 1, March 2006).

the US-led coalition efforts against Daesh. In 2015, Saudi Arabia set up, in haste, an international coalition to intervene in Yemen to degrade the power of the Houthi–Saleh alliance and restore the rule of President Abdrabbuh Mansur Hadi. The idea of a Gulf-led operation launched on its own would have been inconceivable only a few years ago.[3]

This new military assertiveness of Gulf countries is clearly driven by a desire for strategic autonomy. That is not to say strategic independence, but rather the ability to define their security environment on their own terms. Over the past decade, the rapid growth of the UAE as a military player intervening in several regional crises reflects such a major shift. The popular depiction of this federation of seven emirates as a 'little Sparta' – an expression first coined by James Mattis when he was head of CENTCOM – reveals the aspiration of this small state to become a credible security actor.[4]

Although building their own forces has been the primary means of Gulf states to achieve this autonomy, the diversification of international partnerships may also enable them to decrease their reliance on the US and Western countries. This follows the logic of both the emergence of common interests with Asian powers, as demonstrated in the previous chapter, and of hedging against US unpredictability – which means investing in alternative bilateral relations to mitigate a potential risk regarding US military cooperation.

Just as in the case of energy and investment partnerships, the security cooperation between the Arab Peninsula and Asia involves numerous initiatives. This chapter looks at three significant indicators in that respect: the frequency of military-to-military visits and bilateral activities; the use of joint defence industrial projects as an instrument to cement political ties; and the formalisation of cooperation through the signing of MoUs and other bilateral agreements. It argues that although operational exchanges have substantially increased, cooperation at the strategic level remains generally modest, showing that caution endures on both sides in this domain.

The Growth of Military-to-Military Exchanges

Meetings between Asian and Gulf high-level security officials and military representatives have increased considerably since the initiation of the diplomatic momentum described in the previous chapter. These official

---

[3] See Jean-Loup Samaan, *Towards a NATO of the Gulf? The Challenges of Collective Defense Within the GCC* (Carlisle, PA: United States Army War College, 2017).
[4] Rajiv Chandrasekaran, 'In the UAE, the United States has a Quiet, Potent Ally Nicknamed "Little Sparta"', *Washington Post*, 9 November 2014.

visits by senior military leaders, port visits by naval vessels and joint workshops indicate the operationalisation of the relations.

So far, India has been the most active Asian country to promote stronger military-to-military relations with Gulf states. This is the result of India's regional strategy and the fact that the country's strategic thinkers consider the security order in the Arabian Peninsula to be directly linked to India's objectives for South Asia. As India's naval ambitions in the Indian Ocean have grown, its maritime diplomacy in the Gulf has evolved accordingly.[5] In recent years, warships such as the destroyer INS *Delhi* and the frigates INS *Tarkash* and INS *Trikhand* have repeatedly visited the Gulf, stopping in Kuwait, Bahrain, the UAE and Oman. According to Indian officials, the purpose of these deployments is to '[enhance] defence relations and inter-operability with the countries there as well as showing the Indian flag in this region of strategic importance'.[6] In 2008, the Indian Navy also launched a regional initiative to foster maritime cooperation, the Indian Ocean Naval Symposium (IONS).[7] Through various symposia and workshops, IONS brings together the navies of all littoral states – including those of Gulf states.

At the bilateral level, India first developed close military cooperation with Oman. Since 1993, both countries have engaged in a biennial exercise, *Naseem Al Bahr*, which promotes interoperability in several types of missions: surface warfare; air operation; and maritime interdiction operations, as well as Visit Board Search and Seizure.[8] Additionally, the Omani Navy offers berthing and replenishment facilities to India's ships. The Indian Navy is closely monitoring the development of the port of Duqm on Oman's coast, whose location makes it a critical point of access for the navies in the region.[9]

While Oman is India's oldest Gulf partner, it is with the UAE that its military relationship has deepened most dramatically. This follows the logic of the diplomatic momentum between Abu Dhabi and Delhi covered in the previous chapter. The bilateral exchanges between the two countries involve security cooperation, particularly in the field of counterterrorism. The convergence of both countries' threat assessments plays a role here: national security decision-makers in India and the UAE

---

[5] Abhijit Singh, 'The Indian Navy's Arabian Gulf Diplomacy', Institute for Defence Studies and Analyses, IDSA Comment, 24 September 2015.
[6] Rajat Pandit, 'Adding Heft to Diplomacy, India to Send Flotilla of Warships to Persian Gulf', *Times of India*, 24 April 2016.
[7] See <http://www.ions.global/>, accessed on 8 May 2018.
[8] Indian Navy, '"Naseem Al Bahr", a Naval Exercise Between Indian and Oman Navy Held', press release, 25 September 2013.
[9] Sarah Townsend, 'Oman "to Look East" to China, India for Future Investment', *Arabian Business*, 2 October 2017.

support the rapprochement between their countries as they perceive the threat of Islamist terrorism in a similar fashion. In the past, Indian authorities frequently alerted their Emirati counterparts on the flows – human and financial – of terrorist groups from South Asia transiting to Dubai to prepare for their operations on Indian soil. For instance, Dawood Ibrahim, one of the most powerful heads within India's organised-crime sector, who provided logistics for the 2008 Mumbai attacks, lived in Dubai during the 1990s, where many of his real-estate investments were made.[10]

On the UAE side, the government's approach to Islamist movements, and in particular the local branch of the Muslim Brotherhood, Al-Islah, has changed drastically since 2011 as the leadership in Abu Dhabi came to perceive the movement – historically influential in the northern region of the country – as a direct threat to the stability of the federation.[11] Both internally and externally, the UAE pursued a security policy that aimed to prevent the rise of Islamist groups (whether on its own territory, or in Egypt, Libya or Yemen). In January 2017, the attack in Kandahar on a UAE diplomatic delegation to Afghanistan – which killed five diplomats and injured the ambassador – reinforced the firm belief in Abu Dhabi that Islamist groups constitute an existential threat.[12]

This is in line with the view supported in Delhi by Modi's influential national security advisor, Ajit Doval. A former intelligence director, Doval played an instrumental role in hardening India's strategy towards Pakistani terrorist organisations and the indictment of the central authority in Islamabad. He was the architect of the retaliatory strikes against Pakistan in September 2016 which followed the attack against an Indian military base in the Uri district in Kashmir.[13] It is no coincidence that the official statement from the UAE following the attack expressed its full solidarity with India and conveyed its 'support to all actions it may take to confront and eradicate terrorism'.[14]

Security cooperation between the UAE and India also involves the implementation of joint military exercises, such as *Desert Eagle* – a ten-day air combat exercise – which last took place in 2016 at Al-Dhafra base

---

[10] Nistula Hebbar, 'India, UAE Decry State-Sponsored Terror', *The Hindu*, 17 August 2015.

[11] Courtney Freer, 'Rentier Islamism: The Influence of the Muslim Brotherhood in the Gulf', LSE Middle East Centre Paper Series No. 9, November 2015.

[12] Jon Gambrell and Mirwais Khan, 'UAE Mourns 5 Diplomats Killed in Mysterious Afghan Bombing', *Bloomberg*, 11 January 2017.

[13] On Ajit Doval's influence in the Indian national security apparatus, see Praveen Donthi, 'Undercover: Ajit Doval in Theory and Practice', *The Caravan*, 1 September 2017.

[14] Quoted in Dipanjan Roy Chaudhury, 'UAE Supports Indian Action Against Terrorists Post Uri Attacks', *Economic Times*, 3 October 2016.

in Abu Dhabi. Both countries have also convened several naval staff talks since 2007, at which their commanders share lessons learned and discuss good practices in the field of maritime security. Notably, Abu Dhabi hosted an IONS in 2010.

The UAE's growing role in the naval domain is certainly playing a role in India's calculations. As Delhi aims to contain Chinese ambitions in the Indian Ocean, it must become more assertive and rely on strong partnerships with countries bordering its area of influence. In the Arabian Peninsula, the Emirati Navy is one of the few, in terms of capabilities and readiness,[15] to be able to engage in high-intensity maritime operations. This was evidenced by the conduct of Emirati amphibious operations in south Yemen in 2016,[16] the building of UAE naval bases in Eritrea and Somaliland, and the ongoing procurement strategy – which includes *Baynunah*-class corvettes and *Arialah*-class offshore patrol vessels. It is clear that the UAE aims to become a regional maritime player with a presence offshore deep in the Indian Ocean and far beyond its close waters in the Strait of Hormuz.

China also entertains military-to-military relations with the UAE. Chinese and Emirati chiefs of staff and high-level officials have met both in Abu Dhabi and Beijing. In May 2017, Mohammed bin Ahmed Al-Bowardi, minister of state for defence affairs in the UAE, visited China to meet with General Fan Changlong, vice chairman of the Central Military Commission of China, to exchange views on issues 'of mutual interest, especially counter-terrorism efforts, as well as boosting stability and peace'.[17] The information disclosed by official statements on the content of the talks remains limited, but suggests a more modest cooperation compared with that between Abu Dhabi and Delhi.

China has also engaged in a military dialogue with Saudi Arabia. But although the Chinese–Saudi military relations have been acknowledged by both countries as a major area of cooperation, they have not led to significant measures at the operational level, with no concrete measure beyond visits and talks between military authorities. Given the fact that Saudi Arabia had closely worked with China in the 1980s to purchase CSS-2 missiles – which very likely involved a training component – it may seem surprising that more than 20 years later, nothing much has

---

[15] The Omani Navy is also considered a well-trained maritime force, but its capabilities are more limited as a recapitalisation process of its platforms has been launched.

[16] Michael Knights, 'The U.A.E. Approach to Counterinsurgency in Yemen', *War on the Rocks*, 23 May 2016.

[17] *Emirates News Agency*, 'UAE Minister, Chinese Official Discuss Military Cooperation', 17 May 2017.

changed.[18] Taking into consideration the fierce reactions in Washington triggered by the purchase of the CSS-2 missiles, the Saudi leadership may have opted not to exacerbate tensions through deepening its cooperation with China.

South Korea's military cooperation with Gulf states has been modest but still significant, in particular with Oman and the UAE. Indeed, Seoul and Abu Dhabi started building a close military relationship following on from ties first developed in the nuclear and oil sectors. In late 2010, the South Korean government sent a battalion of its special operations forces to the UAE to support the training of Emirati special forces units.[19] The South Korean unit arrived a few months later in the Al-Ain region – 130 km from the capital Abu Dhabi. It comprised 140 soldiers and was symbolically called 'Akh' ('brother' in Arabic). Although the numbers are much smaller than those of American, French or British troops stationed in the UAE, the decision signalled a shift in South Korea's defence diplomacy in general and towards the Gulf in particular. The Akh battalion, one of only four overseas units that Seoul has dispatched, conveys the message that South Korean presence is not only about business prospects but also a commitment to regional stability. In other words, the deployment of South Korean soldiers to the UAE indicates a resolve from both Seoul and Abu Dhabi to expand the previous bilateral programmes and the level of trust that has been achieved to authorise such deployment.

Notably, since 2009 Seoul has deployed another small special naval force, the Cheonghae unit, to the coast of neighbouring Oman, which aims to monitor and combat piracy attacks in the Gulf of Aden.[20]

While this South Korean presence in the UAE and Oman does not attract much attention, the recent announcement of military cooperation between Qatar and Turkey triggered much more speculation. It came to the fore of media coverage during the 2017 crisis between Qatar and its fellow GCC members. Although Turkey offered to act as a mediator, it had already taken significant steps to strengthen military ties with Qatar, in particular with the building of a military base. About 90 Turkish soldiers have already been stationed in Qatar since 2015,[21] and this first Turkish

---

[18] Joseph A Kéchichian, 'Saudi Arabia and China: The Security Dimension', Middle East Institute, 9 February 2016.
[19] *Stratfor Worldview,* 'South Korean Special Operations Forces May Train UAE Troops', 4 November 2010.
[20] *Yonhap News Agency,* 'S. Korea Sends 12th Team of Soldiers to UAE in Military Ties', 10 March 2017.
[21] Antoine Vagneur-Jones and Can Kasapoglu, 'Bridging the Gulf: Turkey's Forward Base in Qatar', *Note de la FRS* (No. 16/2017, 11 August 2017), p. 2.

overseas base since the fall of the Ottoman Empire will eventually be able to hold 3,000 troops. On 7 June, only 48 hours after the initial cut-off of diplomatic relations with the Gulf countries, the Turkish parliament ratified the bilateral defence bill with Qatar, using a fast-track legislative session, and the two countries held their first joint exercise, which included the participation of 250 Turkish soldiers and 30 armoured vehicles.[22] It is worth noting that the size of the Turkish military deployment in Qatar is extremely modest, compared with the US presence in the emirate, which is ten times larger. As of today, it is only slightly bigger than the South Korean unit in the UAE. But numbers are not the primary indicator to follow here. The fact that officials in Ankara and Doha actively publicised the build-up in the midst of the crisis with Gulf neighbours reveals how the Qataris used it as a way to counter narratives of their isolation. The Turkish military 'card' was indeed an effective tool for Doha to claim it had different strategic options, especially regarding the confusion within the US administration. In other words, the Turkish–Qatari military cooperation was a perfect case in point for hedging strategies in practice.

Apart from these cases, military-to-military cooperation remains admittedly modest between the Gulf and the Asian continent. This is the result of political caution as much as the limited military means of countries themselves: apart from Oman, Saudi Arabia and the UAE, the armed forces of the Gulf remain nascent institutions whose readiness has yet to improve. At the military level, countries such as Kuwait and Bahrain still rely heavily on the US and Western powers.

However, overall, given the development of more assertive security policies of both Gulf and Asian countries, the situation could evolve in the future. For instance, a country such as Japan, which has traditionally restricted its armed forces to a defence posture, is raising the scope of its military missions. Abroad, this translates into a new Japanese military diplomacy, evidenced, for instance, by the opening of a military base in Djibouti. Because of Japan's oil and gas trade relations with Gulf countries, it may follow the path of countries such as India and South Korea by strengthening the context of its bilateral dialogues with the GCC member states. At the same time, the more Gulf states modernise their forces and enable them to project power beyond the peninsula, the more they may be willing to improve operational cooperation with Asian partners.

---

[22] Bulent Aras and Pinar Akpinar, *Turkish Foreign Policy and the Qatar Crisis* (Istanbul: Istanbul Policy Center, 2017), p. 4.

The Instrument of Defence Industrial Cooperation

While operational cooperation remains, for the most part, in its infancy, Gulf and Asian countries have used industrial programmes in the military field to foster their bilateral ties. Although Gulf leaders have remained cautious about military-to-military exchanges, they have demonstrated a more confident attitude towards defence industrial cooperation, whose transactional nature may explain the trend. But joint projects on weapons systems and military platform programmes – sometimes involving co-development or offset agreements – also matter because they potentially shape the procurement policies of countries for many years and indicate the ambition of a country to tie the resources of its armed forces to a foreign partner.

As in the field of military-to-military cooperation, Gulf–Asian relations in arms sales largely depend on the maturity of national industries. In this respect, Asian companies are more advanced than those in Gulf states with regard to governance and their defence industrial base. Logically, it is the Saudi and Emirati military industries that have grown in earnest in recent years as decision-makers in Riyadh and Abu Dhabi aspire to progressively rely on their own means.

To be able to build indigenous capabilities, the Saudis and Emiratis have followed a similar trajectory: investing in foreign companies while signing partnerships to produce equipment for their armed forces. This strategy is at play in the Emirati–Indian rapprochement in which the bilateral industrial cooperation targets high-technology areas of specific interest for the UAE armed forces. For instance, the space agencies of both countries, the UAE Space Agency and the Indian Space Research Organisation, started exchanging in 2015. Notably, the launch of an Indian rocket in February 2017, which included 104 nanosatellites, included one from the UAE that had been designed at Sharjah University.[23] With Emirati space ambitions growing – in particular via its emblematic Mars 2117 project[24] – this industrial cooperation is likely to grow.

Likewise, the industrial leg of the bilateral cooperation includes an MoU between Reliance Defence (the military branch of the Indian company Reliance Infrastructure) and Strata Manufacturing, an Emirati company specialising in military aeronautics and fully controlled by Mubadala, one of the two biggest sovereign wealth funds in Abu Dhabi. Although the cooperation only focuses on aeronautic components and its military dimensions are limited, it underlines the extent of the growing

---

[23] Michael Safi, 'India Launches Record-Breaking 104 Satellites from Single Rocket', *The Guardian*, 15 February 2017.
[24] *Gulf News General*, 'UAE to Build First City on Mars by 2117', 14 February 2017.

ties. It is no coincidence that Anil Ambani, the powerful head of Reliance Group, had a personal meeting with Mohammed bin Rashid Al-Maktoum – ruler of Dubai and vice-president of the UAE – on the sidelines of IDEX 2017, the international defence exhibition convened by Abu Dhabi.[25]

Other areas of cooperation are under discussion. In December 2016, the Indian think tank Ananta Centre published a report with the Confederation of Indian Industry on the future of India–UAE economic ties. In the military sector, they identified air and missile defence as a potential area of cooperation, as both countries face similar threats from Iranian or Pakistani ballistic missiles. Additionally, representatives from Abu Dhabi and Delhi have discussed the prospect of the sale of India's Brahmos cruise missiles – initially co-developed with Russia. But as the US remains the primary provider of air defence to the UAE (which has bought Patriot batteries and the Terminal High Altitude Area Defense, THAAD, system), it would be unlikely to observe such a sale without a strong reaction.[26]

Although the hedging dimension remains limited with regard to industrial cooperation with India, it clearly appears in the recent partnership with Russia announced by Abu Dhabi in the field of military aeronautics. In early 2017, the UAE and Russia made public the signing of an initial agreement to develop a light fighter jet – a variation of the MiG-29 – which would be assembled in the UAE.[27] The announcement signalled another significant evolution in the Emirati procurement strategy. As Abu Dhabi has historically relied on American and French military aircraft (such as the F-16 and Mirage-2000), this industrial cooperation with Russia marked both the widening of its geopolitical orientation and the long-term Emirati ambition to become a serious competitor in defence markets.

In some ways, this move towards Russia is the reflection of an industrial strategy that was initiated in the 1990s that has grown in earnest over the past five years.[28] With the formation of the Emirates Defence Industries Company (EDIC) in 2014 – merging the defence activities of three holding companies – the UAE aims to strengthen its engineering and manufacturing capabilities. Although the first objective remains to support the UAE's armed forces, EDIC also sees itself as a future player in the

---

[25] *Khaleej Times*, 'Sheikh Mohammed, Anil Ambani Discuss Defence, Aerospace', 21 February 2017.
[26] Ananta Centre and Confederation of Indian Industry, 'Challenges to the Expansion of India-UAE Economic Ties', 6 December 2016.
[27] Jill Aitoro, 'Russia's Rostec to Co-Develop 5th-Gen Fighter with UAE', *Defense News*, 20 February 2017.
[28] Florence Gaub and Zoe Stanley-Lockman, *Defence Industries in Arab States: Players and Strategies*, Chaillot Paper No. 141 (Paris: European Union Institute for Security Studies, 2017).

global defence market,[29] specifying its desire to expand activities to Southeast Asian countries (Indonesia, Malaysia, Philippines and Thailand, for example) in the production of unmanned aerial vehicles (UAVs).

Saudi Arabia also follows the Emirati path but at a slower pace. Saudi Vision 2030, announced by Crown Prince Mohammed bin Salman in early 2016, plans to concentrate 50 per cent of defence procurement spending inside the kingdom by the end of the next decade. However, the ability of the Saudi industry to match this expectation remains uncertain and will depend on the implementation of concrete measures to build up indigenous capabilities at technological and industrial levels.

As in the UAE, the strengthening of the Saudi defence industry relies on offset agreements,[30] which are included in contracts with Western partners as well as Asian ones. Historically, the hedging calculation has always played a major role in Saudi industrial choices. The leadership in Riyadh has long complained about the difficulties of buying US weapons systems, given the many constraints imposed by Congress.[31] Traditionally, a rejection from Washington regarding arms sales has led Saudi Arabia to look for alternatives among its other Western allies, the UK and France. In the 1990s, the controversial British arms deals with Saudi Arabia, codenamed Al-Yamamah, were originally a response to new US restrictions imposed in the 1980s on exported aircraft.

The same logic applies to Saudi partnerships in Asia, in particular with China. Industrial cooperation with Beijing was initially triggered by President Ronald Reagan's decision to cancel the sale of missiles to Saudi Arabia due to fierce opposition in Congress. As a result, Riyadh turned to Beijing and by 1988, had signed a deal to acquire 50 Dongfeng CSS-2 missiles. Later, the revelation of the sale caused outrage in Washington, especially as the missile was capable of carrying a nuclear payload, a specificity that intensified speculation over Saudi intentions in this field.[32] For Saudi Arabia, the CSS-2 was an effective way to signal to the US that it would not refrain from looking at other options when the US was unable, or

---

[29] International Institute for Strategic Studies, *The Military Balance 2017* (London: Routledge, 2017), p. 354.

[30] Offset agreements can be defined as 'industrial compensation arrangements required by foreign governments as a condition of the purchase of goods and services from nondomestic suppliers'. See Kevin Dehoff, John Dowdy and O Sung Kwon, 'Defense Offsets: From "Contractual Burden" to Competitive Weapon', McKinsey & Company, July 2014.

[31] The most important constraint is the US commitment to Israel's so-called Qualitative Military Edge, which demands that US arms sales to the Middle East not challenge Israeli military superiority in relation to Arab states.

[32] Muhamad S Olimat, *China and the Middle East: From Silk Road to Arab Spring* (London: Routledge, 2013), p. 146.

unwilling, to satisfy its strategic expectations. The same pattern can be observed elsewhere. In 2013, after the US opposed Saudi access to armed UAVs, Riyadh found another solution: it bought China's Wing Loong UAV. A year later, *Newsweek* reported that China had sold DF-21 ballistic missiles to Saudi Arabia in 2007, although neither Beijing nor Riyadh confirmed the information.[33]

Overall, the Chinese share of Saudi arms supplies has always been small. Between 2012 and 2015, Chinese armament transfers to Saudi Arabia came to $600 million, while the US had won contracts worth $17 billion during the same period.[34] Western powers remain the primary origin of Gulf military equipment, but this is as much a consequence of Gulf political partnerships as a choice driven by a comparative industrial assessment. In other words, Gulf countries buy Western equipment also for the technological edge of Western defence companies. However, with Chinese engineering capability growing, for instance, in the aircraft domain with the J-10 and the J-17, this breakdown of arms transfers to the GCC may evolve in the future.

Another illustration of the use of defence deals in Gulf hedging strategies is the latest rapprochement between Saudi Arabia and Russia. In early 2017, King Salman visited Moscow and signed fifteen bilateral agreements, including in the fields of oil, military and space. Among the most significant announcements was an MoU to buy Russia's advanced S-400 long-range air defence system. Although details of the negotiations were discussed by Saudi and Russian officials, the information took the US Department of Defense by surprise, as it had been the traditional provider of Saudi Arabia's air defence. Following the announcement from Russia, Eric Pahon, spokesman for the US Department of Defense, stated, 'We have concerns about the purchasing of the S-400 systems'.[35] The timing was indeed bad for Washington: only one day after King Salman's trip to Moscow, the US State Department announced the awaited approval of a $15-billion contract with Saudi Arabia, which included four THAAD systems.

It is worth noting that operationally, the Saudi purchase of a Russian air defence system hardly makes sense: given the other Western platforms and systems the Saudi forces employ for its territorial defence, the use of

---

[33] See Jeff Stein, 'Exclusive: CIA Helped Saudis in Secret Chinese Missile Deal', *Newsweek*, 29 January 2014. For a cautious assessment of the potential implications of the sale by US authorities, see Ethan Meick, 'China's Reported Ballistic Missile Sale to Saudi Arabia: Background and Potential Implications', US-China Economic and Security Review Commission Staff Report, 16 June 2014.

[34] Catherine A Theohary, 'Conventional Arms Transfers to Developing Nations, 2008-2015', Congressional Research Service, R44716, 2016, p. 36.

[35] Paul McLeary, 'Saudi Dropping Billions on U.S. and Russian Military Hardware', *Foreign Policy*, 6 October 2017.

S-400 missiles could encumber the building of a comprehensive air defence coverage that requires interoperability between the systems. But politically – and despite the 'honeymoon' with the Trump administration – Riyadh sent a strong message to Washington: the kingdom did not feel constrained by its traditional partnership with the US and was comfortable with contemplating cooperation with rival states.

Notably, other Asian countries, such as South Korea and Singapore, play a significant role in Gulf defence markets. For instance, Singapore Technologies (ST) Marine was selected by Muscat for a contract worth $880 million to build four patrol vessels for the Royal Navy of Oman. It was ST Marine's biggest defence export contract and the delivery of this new class of vessels will replace Oman's outdated ships.[36]

Overall, although military industrial cooperation is growing in earnest in the context of Gulf–Asian relations, its scope should not be exaggerated: both regions remain importers rather than exporters of arms and continue to rely primarily on Western companies to fulfil that aim. At this stage, contracts and joint programmes can play a complementary role, but not yet a substitutional one. But it is also in this field that the logic of hedging may be the most salient: for Gulf leaders, arms deals with Russia, China or India might not quantitatively change their portfolios, but they politically allow them to make a stand and assert their autonomy with regard to Western companies and governments that too often consider this regional arms market to be their preserve.

The Meaning of MoUs and Defence Agreements

Formalising a strategic partnership through a written document is the traditional form and the ultimate way to ensure the lasting significance of a relationship. The signing of defence cooperation agreements has in fact been routine for Gulf international policies, especially since the 1991 Gulf War. Gulf regimes have used these documents as a way to bind their fate to the protection of global powers. For instance, Kuwait has signed separate agreements with the five permanent members of the UN Security Council – although the provisions of the agreements differ greatly.

Although defence agreements exist in Asia, they are not as important to regional strategic culture as in the Gulf, and so, in the Gulf–Asian context, bilateral agreements do not have the same function as in Gulf–Western relations. Solidarity clauses and security guarantees are absent and agreements are rather understood as a way to formalise a relationship and build an enduring framework at the working level. This means that

---

[36] *Naval Today*, 'Oman Receives Final Al-Ofouq Patrol Vessel from ST Marine', 27 June 2016.

operational cooperation is encouraged, as long as it does not imply strategic entanglement.

For instance, the bilateral military agreement signed by South Korea and the UAE in January 2010 followed the Emirati decision to award South Korea the contract for their first nuclear plants. The agreement was mostly about technical and operational items and included the transfer of UAVs and other military platforms.[37] In 2017, Seoul signed another military agreement with Bahrain, but its scope was more modest, as it focused on defence procurement and information sharing.

Japan also signed agreements with Bahrain (2012) and Saudi Arabia (2016), which mostly involve exchanges at the working level and between military authorities.[38] Meanwhile, China has been careful not to get enmeshed in Gulf politics, so the documents it has signed are mostly focused on operational cooperation rather than political commitments. As a result, Beijing signed its first military agreement with Kuwait in 1995, followed by a defence and cooperation pact with the UAE in 2008, which mostly focuses on tactical and operational areas of collaboration.[39] The approach with Riyadh was similar: the five-year plan for Saudi–Chinese security cooperation, released in November 2016 by the Saudi government, includes mainly 'counterterrorism cooperation and military drills'.[40] Beijing approved in September 2017 a security cooperation agreement with Qatar that focused primarily on joint counterterrorism activities.[41]

Like other Asian countries, India has been cautious in its approach towards binding agreements, as they go against a traditional foreign policy that emphasises notions of nonalignment and strategic autonomy. Nevertheless, Delhi did play the game of bilateral agreements with Gulf states to achieve the objectives of its 'Look West' policy, signing cooperation agreements with the UAE (2003), Oman (2005), Qatar (2008)

---

[37] Joachim Kolb, 'Small is Beautiful: South Korean-Gulf Relations as an Example of Strategic Engagement by Players in Different Arenas', in Tim Niblock and Monica Malik (eds), *Asia-Gulf Economic Relations in the 21st Century: The Local to Global Transformation* (Berlin: Gerlach Press, 2012), p. 307.

[38] Yukiko Miyagi, 'Japan's Politico-Strategic Relations with the Gulf', in Tim Niblock with Yang Guang, *Security Dynamics of East Asia in the Gulf Region* (Berlin: Gerlach Press, 2014), p. 192.

[39] Muhamad S Olimat, *China and the Middle East Since World War II: A Bilateral Approach* (New York, NY: Lexington, 2014), p. 256.

[40] Samuel Ramani, 'China and Saudi Arabia's Burgeoning Defense Ties', *The Diplomat*, 16 November 2016.

[41] *Gulf Times*, 'Qatar, China Sign Security Pact to Combat Terrorism', 27 September 2017.

and Saudi Arabia (2014).[42] Although the details of each of these agreements may vary, they mostly cover operational matters such as joint training and education programmes. Logically, the 2003 UAE–India defence cooperation agreement is the most advanced. Among several activities, it includes the planning of common military education programmes, the joint production and development of defence equipment, bilateral military exercises and intelligence sharing. It was followed by the setting up of a Joint Committee for Defence Cooperation. In contrast to other bilateral agreements, its scope was much more ambitious, as witnessed by the personal implication of influential figures: Crown Prince Mohammed bin Zayed of Abu Dhabi and the then Chief of General Staff of the UAE Armed Forces were the negotiators.

Even in the case of the much-discussed Turkish–Qatari relationship, the documents made available to the public reveal a rather modest commitment. Beyond the Turkish deployment of troops, the bilateral framework implies a joint committee meeting – equalling a strategic dialogue – that is headed by the Turkish president and the emir of Qatar. But despite much speculation over the Turkish–Qatari defence cooperation, the initial agreement of 2015 does not include a solidarity clause, which would have signalled a pledge in the same way as Qatar's agreements with the US or France.[43] This moderates the view of a Turkish geopolitical shift to the Gulf. While Ankara may look at the agreement as a way to extend its global reach – by supporting economic interests with hard-power capabilities – Doha is unlikely to use the rapprochement as a means of competition towards the US presence. As with its traditional arrangements with international powers, the Qatari leadership will rather consider it an additional layer of regime security.[44] It does not replace the forward headquarters of CENTCOM, but at the political level it balances the conjectural uncertainties about US commitment pledges to the security of the regime. This was what drove the hasty processing of the defence bill by the Turkish parliament.

Similarly, Qatari authorities acknowledged the signing of a military technical cooperation agreement with Russia in late 2017. Although details of the document were not made public, its announcement came with an MoU on air defence and military supplies, domains in which the Qataris traditionally rely on the US.[45] Notably, the agreement was signed just a

---

[42] Prasanta Kumar Pradhan, 'India's Defence Diplomacy in the Gulf', Institute for Defense Studies and Analyses, 27 May 2011.

[43] Vagneur-Jones and Kasapoglu, 'Bridging the Gulf', p. 3.

[44] On the Qatari strategy with international partnerships, see David B Roberts, *Qatar: Securing the Global Ambitions of a City-State* (London: Hurst, 2017).

[45] *Reuters*, 'Qatar, Russia Sign Agreements on Air Defense, Supplies', 26 October 2017.

Table 2: Defence Agreements Between Gulf and Asian Countries

GCC Countries	Asian Countries					
	China	India	Indonesia	Japan	South Korea	Pakistan
Bahrain	None	Under discussion	None	Military Agreement (2012)	Military Agreement (2017)	Military Cooperation Agreement (1971) & Protocol Agreement (1977)
Qatar	Security Cooperation Agreement (2017)	Military Agreement (2008)	None	None	None	Memorandum of Understanding on Defence Cooperation (1983)
Kuwait	Military Agreement (1995)	Under discussion	None	None	None	Defence Cooperation Agreement (1968)
Oman	None	Military Agreement (2005)	None	None	None	Military Cooperation Agreement (1971)
Saudi Arabia	Security Cooperation Plan (2016)	Military Agreement (2014)	Military Agreement (2014)	Military Agreement (2016)	Defence Cooperation Pact (2013)	Mutual Cooperation Program (1967); Military Agreement (2014)
UAE	Defence and Cooperation Pact (2008)	Military Agreement (2003)	Agreement on Defense Industrial Cooperation (2015)	Under discussion	Military Agreement (2010)	Defence Cooperation Agreement (2006)

Note: This list does not aim to be a comprehensive overview of all Asian military relations with Gulf countries. Six Asian countries whose Gulf policy was deemed the most significant were chosen. It is based on open-source information provided by the official authorities of the countries mentioned. The absence of a written document does not imply the absence of military cooperation, but the absence of a publicly known accord in the military field. The entry 'under discussion' indicates ongoing exchanges between countries which have not reached a final agreement at the time of writing.

few weeks after Russia and Saudi Arabia had agreed on the sale of Russian S-400 missile systems.

With regard to Saudi Arabia, the kingdom has signed an impressive number of bilateral agreements involving military matters over the past years. Apart from the above-mentioned cases with Russia and China, it also signed its first defence cooperation agreements with several Asian countries. In early 2014 Riyadh approved agreements with three countries; a first agreement was reached with Pakistan in mid-January,[46] then a week later another with Indonesia. While the agreement with Pakistan suggests that Saudi Arabia can buy fighter jets co-developed by China and Pakistan, the document with Indonesia broadly covers training, education, counterterrorism and defence industry cooperation.[47] Only a month later, it was followed by another MoU, this time between Saudi Arabia and India, which covers military activities in a quasi-identical way to the one with Indonesia.[48]

A comprehensive survey of MoUs and agreements between Asian and Gulf countries may raise questions about the substance of these documents and the resolve of decision-makers to apply their provisions. According to the information made available to the public, they do not constitute binding commitments to the security of each party and therefore do not represent concrete alternatives to the security guarantees offered by Western powers to Gulf states.

However, this does not mean that these initiatives should be dismissed, but rather looked at within the timeframe of the past decade. As in the case of military-to-military exchanges and joint defence industrial projects, the signing of agreements has reshaped diplomatic routines between the Gulf and Asia, creating frameworks and processes that go from strategic dialogue between heads of state to common training for military officers. For the most part, these structures and practices did not exist ten years ago, and although they are certainly no substitute for Gulf–Western security arrangements, they can serve Gulf–Asian common security interests effectively, such as naval cooperation or counterterrorism and intelligence exchanges.

Nevertheless, if the trends of the last decade persist, and if this trend of Gulf–Asian defence relations is to develop further, both sides will face unavoidable dilemmas. As of today, the focus of Gulf countries on operational cooperation, targeting mostly non-state threats such as pirates

---

[46] Although it is worth noting that Saudi Arabia and Pakistan had already signed a military cooperation programme in 1967.
[47] Ankit Panda, 'Indonesia and Saudi Arabia Sign Defense Cooperation Pact', *The Diplomat*, 25 January 2014.
[48] *Ibid*.

and terrorists, is a convenient way to build new partnerships in Asia while sending messages to their traditional Western allies. But eventually, increased military ties would put into question the positions of Gulf and Asian countries regarding the power competition within each region. This is the conundrum explored in the final chapter.

IV. THE FRAGILE DECOUPLING OF REGIONAL POWER PLAYS

While the current intensification of Gulf–Asian relations shows an evolution over the last decade from mere trade exchanges to nascent security cooperation, the eventual outcome of this rapprochement remains uncertain. As the details of these ties mentioned in previous chapters indicate, the hedging approach of Gulf and Asian powers comes from a cautious position.

Decision-makers on both sides have ensured that they do not challenge pre-existing security arrangements, nor do they explicitly target one country. They have refrained from interfering in the issues of the Gulf or the Asian security complexes, in order not to choose one side over the other. In other words, Gulf and Asian powers have tried to build a strategic framework to their relations without being trapped in the classic zero-sum game of alliances.

But hedging without balancing or antagonising is a delicate game that can create confusion, requiring an ability to decouple cooperation with one state from the local power plays in which this state may be involved. This might work on an occasional basis and with a limited scope, but in the long term, strategic relations will inevitably reshape regional security complexes and induce realignments that neither Gulf states nor Asian states seem willing to trigger themselves. This is why there remain some unknowns at the core of new Gulf–Asia geopolitics. This chapter explores three specific conundrums Gulf and Asian countries may face in the near future, each of which would confront them with critical choices.

The first case is India's 'Look West' policy with the Arabian Peninsula, and how it will eventually put into question Gulf historical relations with Pakistan. The second case is Iran–Asia relations. Despite the intensification of their relations with Saudi Arabia and the UAE, countries such as China and India continue to cooperate with Iran in several fields, including energy security and the naval domain. Given the current level of enmity between Tehran and the GCC, any development on Asian–Gulf strategic cooperation will call for a clarification. The third unknown relates to the

US–China global competition and the fact that Gulf states may find themselves in a difficult position, possibly being forced to choose between their traditional security provider and their primary economic partner.

The Future of Gulf–Pakistan Relations

India's strategic engagement with GCC countries may have been in the making for a decade, but it grew in earnest during the mandate of current Prime Minister Narendra Modi. One of the triggers of Modi's policy was the weakening of Gulf ties with Pakistan, following the decision by Islamabad not to join forces with the Saudi-led coalition in Yemen. For Delhi, the Pakistani–Gulf disagreement opened a window of opportunity for stronger cooperation with the peninsula. However, to accurately assess the repercussions of the 2015 crisis, we need to retrace the history of Pakistan's Gulf relations and how they will continue to constrain the rapprochement between the GCC and India.

Gulf political ties with Pakistan are much older than those with India. As far back as 1954, Saudi Arabia's King Saud visited Pakistan and paved the way for a close political relationship.[1] Four years later, Oman ceded the port of Gwadar to Pakistan.[2] Overall, Gulf–Pakistani relations are based on the perception of a common cultural heritage through Islam, while India's treatment of its Muslim minorities has traditionally been seen negatively in the Arabian Peninsula. This sense of a common Islamic identity grew following the formation of the Organisation of the Islamic Conference (now the Organisation of Islamic Cooperation) in 1969. Furthermore, like India, Pakistan represents one of the biggest communities of migrant workers in the Gulf: around 2 million Pakistanis work in Saudi Arabia, with 1.2 million in the UAE.

In addition to these cultural and human dimensions, Gulf–Pakistani relations were for a long time influenced by the Cold War. Whereas India was a partner of the USSR, Islamabad and GCC members were pragmatic supporters of US strategies in the area. As Pakistan's foreign policy was primarily, if not exclusively, driven by its conflict with India, most of its decisions at the international level aimed to counter Delhi's influence. As a result, the US–USSR competition was a convenient narrative for the leadership in Islamabad to benefit from American support and prevent India's engagement with Washington and its Gulf allies.

Similarly, in the 1980s, as the USSR invaded Afghanistan, Saudi Arabia and Pakistan coordinated closely to sponsor and train foreign fighters to

---

[1] Khurram Abbas, 'Pakistan's Relations with Gulf States', Islamabad Policy Research Institute, 4 February 2016.
[2] Nadim Qamar, 'Pakistan and the Persian Gulf', Study Project, US Army War College, 1991, p. 12.

combat Soviet troops. Their assessment of Afghanistan and their purpose differed: from a Saudi perspective, Afghanistan constituted an opportunity to restore its tarnished leadership in the Muslim world after the Iranian Islamic Revolution and the 1979 Siege of Mecca; from Pakistan's perspective, fighting the USSR, a key ally of India, would undermine Delhi's influence on its western border.[3]

This strategic alignment was salient at the level of defence cooperation, as the Pakistani armed forces played a major role in training most of the Gulf's emerging militaries. It is estimated that around 100,000 Pakistanis live in the Kingdom of Bahrain, with many of them serving in local law enforcement.[4] Meanwhile, as Pakistan and Oman share a maritime border, naval cooperation has been frequent and Pakistanis have been sent to train Omani armed forces. However, the outcome of this bilateral programme remained limited due to Oman's own modest military forces.[5] With regard to Qatar, numerous high-level visits took place, and in 2012 both countries signed several agreements on importing LNG, security cooperation and hydroelectric power.

But it is with the UAE and Saudi Arabia that Pakistan's military cooperation has been the strongest. In 1968, Sheikh Zayed, emir of Abu Dhabi and soon to become the founder of the UAE, requested the help of Pakistan's then President Ayub Khan with the training of Abu Dhabi defence forces to replace UK forces, as the latter were initiating their withdrawal. Pakistan's then Air Force Commodore Sadar-ud-Din was appointed Chief of Staff of the Abu Dhabi Air Force. Cooperation intensified after the UAE was established as a unified state in 1971, with training programmes (Pakistan built the UAE Armor Training School) and arms sales. In 1994, a Defence Consultative Group was established to reinforce the institutional framework of the bilateral military relation.[6]

Saudi–Pakistan military relations date back to the early 1960s. In 1963, the Pakistani military initiated contacts with Saudi authorities to offer security assistance. Pakistan's military presence within the Arab world was so active at that time that the Pakistan Air Force (PAF) went as far as to send personnel

---

[3] Frédéric Grare, *Pakistan and the Afghan Conflict 1979-1985* (Karachi: Oxford University Press, 2003).

[4] *Strategic Comments*, 'India and Pakistan's Evolving Relationships with the Gulf' (Vol. 22, No. 7, 2016); Sehar Kamran, *Pak-Gulf Defense and Security Cooperation* (Rawalpindi: Center for Pakistan and Gulf Studies, 2013), p. 13.

[5] Muhammad Anwar, *Friends Near Home: Pakistan's Strategic Security Options* (Bloomington, IN: AuthorHouse, 2006), p. 96.

[6] Kamran, *Pak-Gulf Defense and Security Cooperation*, p. 4.

to combat missions during the 1967 Arab–Israeli War.[7] In addition, the PAF shored up the Royal Saudi Air Force in its campaign against Soviet-backed South Yemen in 1969. In return for this Pakistani operational support, the kingdom provided financial aid to Pakistan, supplying fighter aircraft two years later during the war with India that led to the traumatic secession of East Pakistan, which then became Bangladesh. Later, Pakistani troops assisted Saudi Arabia in the Siege of Mecca in 1979.

Furthermore, Saudi financial support to Pakistan continued to increase. By the mid-1970s, it amounted to $500 million – representing 25 per cent of total Saudi aid.[8] While Saudi Arabia was transferring funds, Pakistan was deploying troops: more than 3,000 military advisers were sent in the early 1980s to Saudi Arabia, increasing to 40,000 during the following years.[9] The Gulf War of 1990–91 further evidenced Pakistan's security provisions to the Arab Gulf states, as Islamabad supported the coalition against the Iraqi invasion of Kuwait and deployed troops to protect holy sites in Saudi Arabia.[10]

But the most intriguing part of Saudi–Pakistani military relations relates to the international suspicions over their cooperation in the nuclear field. Pakistan's nuclear programme grew rapidly in the 1980s at the same time as Saudi Arabia acquired CSS-2 ballistic missiles from China, which were considered potential delivery systems. Although no concrete evidence nor official statement from the parties suspected have ever been made public, there have been regular accusations and US officials have occasionally expressed concern over Saudi official visits to Pakistan's nuclear plants.[11] Despite Saudi dismissal of the suspicions, US newspapers have regularly claimed that they have found evidence, based on 'Pakistani insiders', of a secret agreement on nuclear cooperation, under which Pakistan would provide Saudi Arabia with nuclear technology in return for

---

[7] William Staudenmaier and Shirin Tahir-Kheli, 'The Saudi-Pakistan Military Relationship and its Implications for US Strategy in Southeast Asia', Special Report, US Army War College, 1981, p. 2.

[8] Adeed Dawisha, *Saudi Arabia's Search for Security*, Adelphi Paper, No. 158 (London: International Institute for Strategic Studies, 1980), p. 18.

[9] Staudenmaier and Tahir-Kheli, 'The Saudi-Pakistan Military Relationship and its Implications for US Strategy in Southeast Asia', p. 11.

[10] P B Sinha, 'The Gulf War and Pakistan', *Strategic Analysis* (Vol. 4, No. 7, 1980), pp. 295–300.

[11] In 1999, US officials expressed concern about a visit by Prince Sultan, the Saudi defence minister, to the uranium enrichment facility at Kahuta and the missile facility at Ghauri in Pakistan. During the visit, Prince Sultan also met with A Q Khan, the now infamous nuclear scientist responsible for the dissemination of critical information and technologies related to nuclear proliferation. See Gordon Corera, *Shopping for Bombs: Nuclear Proliferation, Global Insecurity, and the Rise and Fall of the A.Q. Khan Network* (Oxford: Oxford University Press, 2006).

oil at reduced prices.[12] However, independent observers have challenged the belief of a Pakistani 'extended deterrence' option to Saudi Arabia by emphasising that such a scenario is operationally dubious, in part because Pakistan's arsenal is 'focused entirely on India'.[13]

Overall, Pakistan entertained a long and close relationship with Gulf countries, which logically prevented any significant cooperation between the latter and India. In fact, the shift in Gulf ties with Pakistan came as a result of Islamabad's decision not to participate in Operation *Decisive Storm* led by Riyadh in Yemen in 2015.[14] The repercussions of Pakistan's rebuttal were mostly felt in Saudi Arabia and the UAE, which had not only been Pakistan's closest partners in the Gulf, but were also by far the biggest contributors of the military coalition in Yemen.

The context in Islamabad at the time of the decision is important: following a fierce debate in parliament, the Pakistani government decided to stay neutral, expressing doubts about the strategic objectives of the intervention and its implementation. Additionally, commentators argued that China may have pressured Pakistan's then Prime Minister Nawaz Sharif not to get entangled in a regional conflict, as Beijing was announcing investments totalling $47 billion in the country as part of BRI loans and projects.[15] Finally, Pakistani leaders may have feared that their participation in a Saudi-led campaign against Yemen's Houthis would stir discontent within Pakistan's Shia minority. In order to assuage Saudi pressures, Islamabad offered military support to secure Saudi borders against potential attacks launched from Yemen, but it ultimately failed to reassure its Gulf partners. Pakistan's position was followed by numerous expressions of outrage in the Gulf: Anwar Gargash, UAE minister of state for foreign affairs, described the decision as 'inconsistent, dangerous and unexpected', adding that Pakistan would pay a 'heavy price [for its] ambiguous stand'.[16] The Gulf media conveyed a similar message of condemnation, shaming the Pakistanis for their abandonment. In the Pakistani province of Khyber Pakhtunkhwa, the construction of an oil refinery planned by the Emirati company Xcelera Resources (valued at

---

[12] *Washington Times*, 'Pakistan, Saudi Arabia in Secret Nuke Pact', 21 October 2003.
[13] Mark Fitzpatrick, 'Saudi Arabia, Pakistan and the Nuclear Rumour Mill', *Survival* (Vol. 57, No. 4, 2015).
[14] Louis Ritzinger, 'Why Pakistan is Staying Out of Yemen', *National Interest*, 27 April 2015.
[15] For the Chinese factor in Pakistan's decision, see Ankit Panda, 'Pakistan's Neutrality in the Yemen Crisis: Brought to You by China', *The Diplomat*, 28 April 2015; Kamran Yousaf, 'Defying Royal Request: China Helped Pakistan "Weather the Storm" over Yemen', *Express Tribune*, 27 April 2015.
[16] *Pakistan Today*, 'UAE Warns Pakistan of "Heavy Price for Ambiguous Stand" on Yemen', 12 April 2015.

$500 million) was subsequently suspended. But the damage to UAE–Pakistan relations proved to be the worst. Along with Saudi Arabia, the UAE had provided Pakistan with development aid for several decades and perceived Islamabad's decision on Yemen as ungrateful.[17] Pakistan had been, after all, a major recipient of UAE aid after the 2005 Kashmir earthquake and the displacement of the region's population.

In addition to the Yemen issue, UAE–Pakistan relations also worsened because of the latter's policy in Afghanistan. As Emirati forces were sent to Afghanistan, the influence of Islamabad on local Islamist militias had direct consequences for the UAE. On 10 January 2017, an attack against Emirati diplomats in Kandahar killed five and injured the UAE's ambassador to Afghanistan (he died a few weeks later).[18] Afghan forces quickly claimed that the Taliban, operating from Quetta inside Pakistan, were responsible for the attack, which was immediately denied by the Taliban, but which further damaged relations between Islamabad and Abu Dhabi.[19] It reinforced the Emirati perception that the Sharif government was too accommodating with Islamist movements operating on its soil.[20]

In this context of high tensions, it is obvious that the Indian outreach to the Gulf caused concern in Islamabad. Nevertheless, it did not yet translate into a clear strategic realignment from GCC countries. Notably, Saudi Arabia seemed not to favour a complete rift. In January 2017, Riyadh nominated Raheel Sharif, former chief of the Pakistani army, as the first commander of the Islamic Military Alliance, a new organisation created by Saudi Crown Prince Mohammed bin Salman in 2015. The nomination was remarkable, given the past responsibilities of Sharif in the Pakistani military apparatus, and indicated Riyadh's enduring proximity with Pakistan's military. Nevertheless, the exact responsibilities of the position have not yet been made clear.

In addition to Sharif's appointment, the Pakistani government announced in March 2017 that consultations with Saudi Arabia were to be held to deploy a brigade of its combat troops to the kingdom, more precisely at the Saudi–Yemeni border. Pakistani officials, such as Defence Minister Khawaja Asif, were cautious not to describe the talks as a revision of their policy on the war in Yemen: the Pakistani brigade would operate

---

[17] Ayesha Almazroui, 'Why is Pakistan not Supporting its Old Friend at this Critical Time?', *The National*, 12 April 2015.

[18] Gambrell and Khan, 'UAE Mourns 5 Diplomats Killed in Mysterious Afghan Bombing'.

[19] Ruchi Kumar, 'UAE Ambassador Returns Home for Treatment After Bombing in Kandahar', *The National*, 12 January 2017.

[20] Emile Hokayem and Rahul Roy-Chaudhury, 'India and the UAE: Towards Strategic Cooperation', International Institute for Strategic Studies, 23 January 2017.

strictly inside Saudi Arabia. Overall, the measure worked as a reassurance signal sent to the rulers in Riyadh.

Pakistan's long military influence in the Gulf poses the Gulf states with a delicate dilemma. Nurturing ties with both Delhi and Islamabad works as long as it is not perceived by one or the other as threatening. But if military cooperation increases in fields such as naval exercises and counterterrorism – as the agreements between India and the Gulf states envision – this could trigger a reaction from Pakistan, as it is inevitable that Islamabad would feel encircled by a Gulf–India rapprochement. GCC members, as Western countries before them, will not be left out of this equation. Pakistan's political and military leadership is therefore susceptible to pressure from its partners in the Arabian Peninsula not to take measures that could – in Islamabad's perception – jeopardise the status quo in South Asia. The problem is that Pakistan's political and financial leverage with Gulf countries is modest. It cannot economically coerce the Arab monarchies and the recent US–India rapprochement has changed the geopolitical environment that initially favoured Islamabad during the Cold War. This is why some states, such as the UAE, may consider a gradual shift, while others – possibly Saudi Arabia – might try to accommodate relations with both Pakistan and India by slowing down the pace of a rapprochement with the latter.

Asia and the Gulf–Iran Rivalry

Current Gulf–Iran relations may have reached their lowest point since the Islamic Revolution of 1979, as they have now turned the confrontation between Tehran and Riyadh into the defining power struggle of the Middle East. Nevertheless, so far this does not seem to have affected relations between Asian countries and Iran. Iranian policy towards Asia has not suffered significantly from tensions with its Gulf neighbours, and in fact, the country still enjoys stable relations, particularly with India and China.

Iran's Asia policy is driven by geographic proximity and trade opportunities as much as the absence of other major geopolitical options. The rise of the Islamic Republic in 1979 and the hostage crisis at the US Embassy in Tehran the same year marked a complete reorientation of Iran's international relations. Under the new regime, Iran's foreign policy followed a non-Western posture. In the context of the Cold War, former Iranian Supreme Leader Ayatollah Khomeini and his close circle put an end to the Iranian–American partnership, but without embracing the USSR. Given the legacy of Russia–Iran disputes, in particular in Central Asia, the Islamic Republic of Iran designed a foreign policy that viewed Russia with suspicion and only occasionally supported its regional policies when they aligned with its own interests.[21] The tenets of this Iranian policy endured, especially after the outbreak of the 2003 crisis over its clandestine nuclear programme. Being sanctioned and isolated by Western powers, Iran faced the problem of its foreign policy partnerships in a completely different way from the GCC countries: it was not about diversifying its options, but rather avoiding complete isolation from international players.

Tehran prevented this outcome by cultivating economic and military ties with Asian countries, in particular China and India, even though the relations were complex. Despite the economic sanctions imposed on Iran, India maintained significant trade relations with Tehran, especially because of Indian oil imports from Iran. In Mangalore, the chief port city of Karnataka state, India has stored strategic oil reserves (approximately 6 million barrels) supplied by Iran – interestingly, the UAE committed to the shipment of similar reserves to the same location.[22] In return, India has been investing in the construction of the Chabahar port and the Farzad-B oil fields in southeast Iran.

When it comes to these projects, India's calculations have less to do with competition between Iran and the Gulf than with its own rivalry with Pakistan: Chabahar is located 80 km from the Pakistani port of Gwadar, whose construction has been supported by China – an estimated $54-billion budget is planned. Under the current circumstances, Gwadar would be one of the key gateways in China's BRI.[23]

At the same time, Indian officials frequently complain about Iranian business practices, which are marked by constant political interference and repeated renegotiations of contracts. In the recent past, Iranian authorities cancelled a contract for the export of LNG to India as a retaliatory measure following India's vote against the Iranian nuclear programme at the International Atomic Energy Agency.[24]

Although business relations are complicated, military cooperation has been steadier. Both countries share a security interest with regard to the Indian Ocean, and, despite Western and Gulf discontent, the Indian Navy invites Iran to the various activities of its IONS. Additionally, Iran and India have cooperated on the Afghanistan issue and, in the mid-1990s,

---

[21] Clément Therme, *Les relations entre Téhéran et Moscou depuis 1979* (Paris: Presses Universitaires de France, 2013).

[22] Sanjay Dutta, 'First Abu Dhabi Oil to Flow for Mangalore Storage by May', *Times of India*, 13 February 2018.

[23] Henny Sender and Kiran Stacey, 'China Takes "Project of the Century" to Pakistan', *Financial Times*, 17 May 2017.

[24] Sandeep Joshi, 'India Looks Beyond Iran to Boost its Crude Oil Supplies', *The Hindu*, 16 June 2012.

shared similar concerns over the rise of the Taliban – which at that time had been recognised by Saudi Arabia and the UAE.

Iran also entertains good relations with China, dating back to the beginning of the Islamic Republic, when China became the primary supplier of arms to Iran, due to the dual distance established by the Khomeini regime towards the US and the USSR. At the economic level, China remains the most important buyer of Iranian oil. Iran provides 12 per cent of Chinese annual oil consumption, while China represents a third of Iran's overall trade. In the 2000s, China poured money into the maintenance and upgrading of Iran's three oil refineries,[25] and Iran's state-owned North Drilling Company has a close relationship with China National Petroleum Corporation (CNPC). In 2009, as relations with French company Total deteriorated – over seeming delays in the development of Iran's South Pars Gas Project – Tehran decided to replace it with a consortium composed of CNPC and Malaysia's Petronas. The new deal was worth $4.7 billion.[26]

Following the 2003 crisis over Iran's clandestine nuclear programme, China's attitude towards the international sanctions against Tehran was ambivalent. Unconvinced by the danger of Iranian nuclear ambitions, Beijing dismissed the sanctions, and while Japanese and European companies removed their assets in the late 2000s, China continued to make significant deals, for instance in the oil extraction sector in the Iranian regions of North Azadegan and Yadavaran.[27] In 2015, sanctions against Iran were lifted just a week before President Xi travelled to Iran and made a pledge to increase bilateral trade to $600 billion.[28] Similarly, in September 2017, while President Trump was threatening to renegotiate the nuclear deal with Iran, China's CITIC investment group provided Iranian banks with a loan of $10 billion.[29] Moreover, even though Iranian exports to China decreased – due to Beijing's compliance with the UN Security Council sanctions regarding Iran's nuclear programme – five years later, China's consumption of Iranian oil had surged and it is estimated that it will now reach a record.[30]

---

[25] Olimat, *China and the Middle East*, p. 159.

[26] *Ibid.*, p. 158.

[27] Willem van Kemenade, 'China vs. the Western Campaign for Iran Sanctions', *Washington Quarterly* (Vol. 33, No. 3, July 2010), pp. 99-114; Christina Lin, 'The East Asian Loophole in Iran Sanctions: Encouraging Compliance by Our Allies and China', Policywatch 1689, Washington Institute for Near East Policy, 12 August 2010.

[28] Kenneth Katzman, 'Iran's Foreign and Defense Policies', Congressional Research Service, R44017, 22 September 2017, p. 51.

[29] *Tehran Times*, 'Iran Secures $10 Billion Chinese Funding', 15 September 2017.

[30] Chen Aizhu, 'China's Iran Oil Imports to Hit Record on New Production: Sources', *Reuters*, 5 January 2017.

In conjunction with Iran's energy exports to China, the country's location makes it a potential hub for China's BRI. In fact, Chinese workers are already involved in the improvement of Iranian infrastructure, such as railroads and bridges, which would connect the country to Turkmenistan and Afghanistan. The Tehran–Mashhad railroad has been financed with a $1.6-billion loan from China.[31] A new line to connect Urumqi in the western region of Xinjiang to Tehran (a distance of 3,500 km) is planned to open in 2021.

The China–Iran connection also has significant military ramifications. In November 2016, both countries signed a military cooperation agreement that includes initiatives such as military training and counterterrorism operations. Following the agreement, Iran's then Defence Minister Hossein Dehghan told the press, '[t]he upgrading of relations and long-term defense-military cooperation with China is one of the main priorities of the Islamic Republic of Iran's defense diplomacy'.[32]

China has been an active provider of military technology to Iran for years, including tactical ballistic and anti-ship cruise missiles, advanced anti-ship mines and Houdong fast-attack boats, which the Iranian Revolutionary Guard Corps deploy in the Gulf. Notably, the anti-ship missile that Lebanon's Hizbullah used against the Israeli corvette INS *Hanit* during the 2006 war was a Chinese-designed C-802 'Silkworm' cruise missile that had been transferred to the organisation by the Iranians. Moreover, according to US authorities, Iran also supplied Yemeni Houthi insurgents with Chinese-made man-portable surface-to-air missiles (MANPADs).[33]

When questioned about these problematic transfers, the Chinese authorities defend themselves by pointing out loopholes in the monitoring of dual technology transfers. But given the proximity of the suppliers to the Chinese state, their argument is questionable. In the past, US sanctions directly targeted Chinese entities responsible for providing support to Iran's ballistic missile programme, including major groups such as the China National Precision Machinery Import and Export Corporation, which is owned by the state. There have even been speculations within the US government that China may have played a facilitating role in Iran–North Korea cooperation in the military field. As a provider of sensitive technology and hardware to both countries, Beijing was certainly in the

---

[31] Thomas Erdbrink, 'For China's Global Ambitions, "Iran is at the Center of Everything"', *New York Times*, 25 July 2017.

[32] Franz-Stefan Gady, 'Iran, China Sign Military Cooperation Agreement', *The Diplomat*, 15 November 2016.

[33] Christopher Harmer, 'Iranian Naval and Maritime Strategy', Middle East Security Report No. 12, Institute for the Study of War, June 2013, p. 22.

right position to have detailed knowledge of the exchanges between Tehran and Pyongyang.[34]

Although arms sales were initiated in the early 1980s, military-to-military cooperation started much later and focused primarily on the maritime domain. In 2013, Iranian warships visited the port city of Zhangjiagang in China's Jiangsu province, the first time Iranian maritime forces entered the Pacific Ocean.[35] A four-day naval exercise was then organised in September 2014, with two Chinese warships docking at Iran's port of Bandar Abbas. This was a significant step, in particular given the fact that only a few years before, the Chinese Navy would not have felt confident enough to sail warships in the area.[36] In 2015, the commander of the Islamic Republic of Iran Navy, Habibollah Sayyari, made a visit to China, another unprecedented step. In June 2017, Iran and China conducted another joint naval exercise in the Gulf in the midst of increased tensions between Washington and Tehran related to Iran's latest ballistic missile tests and arms transfers to the Houthis in Yemen. Even though this last exercise was modest in scope and involved primarily one Iranian destroyer and two Chinese destroyers,[37] China's participation reflected the resolve of Beijing to sustain its military cooperation with Iran despite the numerous crises in the Gulf.

Additionally, Iran's potential membership of the Shanghai Cooperation Organisation (SCO) and China's support of its application is another reflection of bilateral ties.[38] Iran's application for full SCO membership had been on the agenda for almost a decade since April 2008 when the country had expressed its intent to join. Initially, the membership was rejected because of UN Security Council sanctions against Iran, but in 2015 the JCPOA removed this constraint and at the 2017 Summit held in Astana, the SCO announced that India's and Pakistan's membership had been formally accepted. Iran's membership would strengthen its inclusion in Asian diplomatic arrangements.

How have Gulf Arab states reacted to these developments in Iran–Asian relations? So far, these have not been on the agenda of Gulf talks with their Asian counterparts. Although Saudi Arabia increasingly puts pressure on its partners to isolate Iran and to apply the zero-sum rule,

[34] Shirley Kan, 'China and Proliferation of Weapons of Mass Destruction and Missiles: Policy Issues', Congressional Research Service, 5 January 2015, p. 18.
[35] Harmer, 'Iranian Naval and Maritime Strategy', p. 21.
[36] Mustafa Salama, 'Navy Exercises Bring Iran, China Closer', *Al Monitor*, 19 October 2014.
[37] *Reuters*, 'Iran and China Conduct Naval Drill in Gulf', 18 June 2017.
[38] Founded in 2001 for border security, counterterrorism and the fight against drug trafficking, the Shanghai Cooperation Organisation includes China, Russia, Kazakhstan, Kyrgyzstan, Tajikistan and Uzbekistan.

most of the smaller GCC members remain pragmatic regarding the isolation of Iran. Dubai remains the transit point for Iranian companies to access global markets, Qatar shares with Iran the largest gas field in the world (South Pars-North Dome field),[39] and Oman maintains open relations with the regime in Tehran.

Gulf reactions to Iran–Asia relations have also been restrained because Tehran's policies towards Asian partners themselves are unstable. Iran may benefit from Asian investments, but it does not embrace the security agendas of Asian partners. While India may see its investment in Chabahar as a tactical counterweight to Gwadar, representatives in Tehran downplay this strategic significance. Therefore the governor of the Iranian province of Sistan and Baluchistan, Ali Oset Hashemi, agreed with the chief minister of Pakistan's Balochistan, Nawab Sanaullah Zehri, to make Gwadar and Chabahar 'sister port cities'.[40]

Iran–Pakistan relations themselves have been going through some complicated phases. The countries are in the process of discussing a joint gas pipeline project, which initially involved India until Delhi decided in 2009 to abandon it, claiming that the security of the pipeline could not be adequately guaranteed. Iran built the line on its side of the border, while Pakistan did not due to financial limitations, but by mid-2015, China had agreed to help Pakistan by investing $2 billion in the pipeline. In the 1990s, a close Iranian–Pakistani military cooperation existed, and Abdul Qadeer Khan, a key figure in Pakistan's nuclear programme, sold nuclear technology and designs to Iran.[41] Later, Pakistan's support for the Afghan Taliban created a rift with Tehran. Moreover, Iranian Sunni Muslim militias targeting the Iranian regime, such as Jundullah and Jaysh Al-Adl, reportedly operate from western Pakistan.[42]

Conversely, other Asian countries, such as Japan and South Korea, have remained cautious about their relations with Iran and have not engaged in military cooperation like India, Pakistan and China. Commercial relations exist and the oil trade increased following the lifting of international sanctions against Iran, but for various reasons Japan and South Korea are unlikely to develop ties with Iran. It is worth noting that no Japanese prime minister has visited Iran since the birth of the Islamic Republic in 1979. Prime Minister Shinzo Abe was initially expected to

---

[39] Alex Vatanka, 'The Odd Couple: Iran and Qatar: Two Regional Misfits', *The Majalla*, 22 March 2012.
[40] Kabir Taneja, 'The Reality of India-Iran Ties', *The Diplomat*, 11 July 2016.
[41] Bruno Tertrais, 'Not a "Wal-Mart", but an "Imports-Exports Enterprise": Understanding the Nature of the A.Q. Khan Network', *Strategic Insights* (Vol. 6, No. 5, August 2007).
[42] Katzman, 'Iran's Foreign and Defense Policies', p. 47.

travel there in August 2016, but the visit was postponed with no specific indication of a future date.

Specifically, the Iranian–North Korean cooperation on weapons of mass destruction and ballistic missiles reduces the incentives for closer exchanges, given the threat Pyongyang still constitutes for Tokyo and Seoul. The proximity of both countries to the US – much more important than to India – and their reliance on the US military for their security prevent them from moving towards Iran.

Iran's Asia policy may become a more polarising issue than that of Pakistan in the equation of Gulf–Asian relations. Given the increased sensitivity of Gulf rulers to Tehran's regional policies, they may consider Asian military activities with Iran unacceptable. The fact that some Iranian military technologies used in the Gulf, or transferred to proxies such as Hizbullah and the Houthis, derive from Chinese transfers to Iran certainly fuels discontent in the Gulf. Eventually, for countries such as India and China, the cost of relations with Iran would become greater than the profit. Given the stake of energy imports and investment projects with the Gulf, the economic and political gains from engaging with Tehran would clearly not be worth losing. But at the same time, this would mean an increase in Asian reliance on the Arabian Peninsula for its oil and gas supplies, which may prevent them from fully tilting the scales.

US–China Competition and the Limits of Gulf Hedging Strategies

The last major limit of diplomatic diversification for Gulf policies relates to the position of these countries regarding US–China competition. Increasingly, the international relations of Gulf states will be shaped by two distinct – and potentially contradictory – pillars: their economic wealth will rely on China's global rise while their political survival may be ensured, at least for the time being, by US security provisions. This equation would not qualify as a contradiction if both the US and China were allies or partners, but the bilateral relationship is moving in the other direction. President Barack Obama's tenure and the first two years of the Trump presidency were marked by a steady deterioration of the dialogue between Washington and Beijing and the growing perception that both countries are leaning towards rivalry rather than cooperation.[43]

---

[43] Aaron L Friedberg, *A Contest for Supremacy: China, America, and the Struggle for Mastery in Asia* (New York, NY: W W Norton, 2011); Ashley J Tellis, 'Balancing Without Containment: A U.S. Strategy for Confronting China's Rise', *Washington Quarterly* (Vol. 36, No. 4, Fall 2013); Robert D Blackwill and Ashley J Tellis,

US–China relations are important for Gulf countries both at global and regional levels. At the global level, competition between the US and China could potentially reshape alliances and partnerships in a way that is reminiscent of the Cold War era. Since 2012, the presidency of Xi Jinping has been marked by a reinvigorated Chinese assertiveness. Chinese 'gunboat diplomacy' in the South China Sea, regarding claims to islands that are disputed by its Asian neighbours, triggered a firm response from Washington to reassure its local allies of its support, while the global ambitions of Beijing were perceived as new hegemonic ambitions.[44] The US 'pivot' initiated by Barack Obama – and likely to expand under Trump – consisted of a mix of increased military resources allocated to the Pacific Command and a stronger public commitment to the Asian security system. Eventually, the 'pivot' signalled the growing containment mindset that was shaping Washington's policies on Beijing.

This evolution of US–Chinese relations into a global competition obviously has an impact on all Asian countries. For instance, in light of China's rise, India recalibrated its economy-oriented 'Look East' policy to include a strategic dimension.[45] Japan and Australia increased their national security resources and strengthened their ties to the US to prevent being overwhelmed by China's ascendancy.[46] Other smaller countries in the Asian security environment, such as ASEAN members, have been more ambivalent about China's rise and have kept their distance regarding the US pivot in order not to antagonise Beijing. In fact, this was already a case study of strategic hedging,[47] but Gulf states are comparatively much more closely aligned to the US than ASEAN members when it comes to security and defence policies. Therefore, while a country such as Vietnam can still play the hedging game – especially as it shares a border with China – it may become increasingly difficult for a country such as Qatar, hosting the forward headquarters of CENTCOM, to

---

Revising U.S. Grand Strategy Toward China (New York, NY: Council on Foreign Relations, 2015).

[44] Christian Le Mière, 'The Return of Gunboat Diplomacy', *Survival* (Vol. 53, No. 5, 2011).

[45] Grare, *India Turns East*.

[46] Yuki Tatsumi (ed.), 'US-Japan-Australia Security Cooperation: Prospects and Challenges', Stimson Center, April 2015; Hugh White, *Power Shift: Australia's Future Between Washington and Beijing* (Collingwood: Quarterly Essay, 2010); William Tow et al. (eds), *Asia-Pacific Security: US, Australia and Japan and the New Security Triangle* (New York, NY: Routledge, 2007).

[47] Medeiros, 'Strategic Hedging and the Future of Asia-Pacific Stability'; Robert S Ross, 'Balance of Power Politics and the Rise of China: Accommodation and Balancing in East Asia', *Security Studies* (Vol. 15, No. 3, 2006); Evelyn Goh, 'Southeast Asian Perspectives on the China Challenge', *Journal of Strategic Studies* (Vol. 30, Nos 4–5, 2007).

ignore US global priorities. This is where the strategic hedging logic behind the Gulf rapprochement with Asia could translate into loose, if not fuzzy, arrangements.

It is worth contemplating here the idea that Gulf states may consider their rapprochement with China to be a serious endeavour. In the short term, this hedging posture allows them to increase their level of strategic autonomy with regard to their traditional Western partners, but in the long term it paves the way for deep contradictions: how could Arab kingdoms build strong ties with China – at political and military levels – while the latter may be engaged in a conflict with their primary security provider, namely the US?

The same is true of Gulf–India relations. If tensions increase between Delhi and Beijing, or if a conflict occurs between the two, Gulf countries such as Saudi Arabia and the UAE may have to make a choice. As economic ties translate into political dialogues, it becomes much more difficult to avoid taking a stand one way or the other. The eagerness of these Gulf states to position themselves as active partners to both Indian and Chinese regional projects is sustainable as long as relations between the latter do not turn into open hostility. It is worth remembering that China's BRI could render India's regional projects, such as its 'Look East' policy, irrelevant. In other words, Gulf investments in Asia may be driven by economic prospects, but they will eventually impact the regional balance of power.

China's Gulf states policy will also matter at the regional level, because of the expansion of China's military presence in the Indian Ocean and the Gulf itself. Currently, US defence officials do not look at the Gulf security complex and China's presence in the Indian Ocean as two parts of a single, coherent strategic challenge. This is partly due to the bureaucratic division of labour within the US Department of Defense – Gulf countries are covered by CENTCOM, China by the Pacific Command – but this may change. China's deployment of warships in the area and the construction of a base in Djibouti – close to Saudi Arabia's – are changing the way those in US policy circles look at the region.[48] In the Pentagon, experts believe that in the future, 'China most likely will seek to establish additional military bases in countries with which it has a longstanding

---

[48] Bertil Lintner, 'A New Cold War in the Indian Ocean?', *National Interest*, 19 June 2017; Daniel Stacey and Alastair Gale, 'China Races Ahead in Indian Ocean While India and Japan Take Baby Steps', *Wall Street Journal*, 23 July 2017; Peter Dombrowski and Andrew C Winner (eds), *The Indian Ocean and US Grand Strategy: Ensuring Access and Promoting Security* (Washington, DC: Georgetown University Press, 2014).

friendly relationship and similar strategic interests'.[49] In other words, the Arabian Peninsula could, in the not so distant future, become a potential location for Chinese overseas deployments. This hypothetical Chinese military footprint would logically complement the BRI, a phenomenon which, for independent observers in Washington, requires the US to 'take more seriously the strategic challenges posed by China's OBOR [BRI] initiative'.[50] As a result, Gulf countries may not be able to ignore the US–China strategic equation indefinitely.

The outcome of this equation would imply numerous scenarios of critical importance for GCC countries. Washington could openly oppose Chinese–Gulf strategic cooperation similarly to the way they pressured their European allies and Israel in the past not to engage in military exchanges that might indirectly challenge US military posture in Asia.[51] If tensions escalate in the Pacific Ocean, the US may also find its military commitments – globally and in the Arabian Peninsula in particular – unsustainable for financial reasons or political ones. Policy ideas such as 'selective engagements' may resurface to drive US global posture.[52] Already, the salience of the 'America First' rhetoric used by Donald Trump is testimony of the enduring seduction of US isolationist views and could foretell a future decrease of the American footprint in the region.[53]

---

[49] US Department of Defense, 'Military and Security Developments Involving the People's Republic of China 2017', Annual Report to Congress, 15 May 2017, p. 4.

[50] Ashley Tellis, 'Protecting American Primacy in the Indo-Pacific', testimony to the Senate Armed Services Committee, 25 April 2017.

[51] On Europe–China relations, see David Murphy and Shada Islam, 'China's Love Affair with Europe', *Far Eastern Economic Review* (February 2004), pp. 26–29; May-Britt U Stumbaum, *Risky Business? The EU, China and Dual-Use Technology*, European Union Institute for Security Studies Occasional Paper No. 80 (Paris: European Union Institute for Security Studies, 2009); Hugo Meijer, *Transatlantic Perspectives on China's Military Modernization: The Case of Europe's Arms Embargo Against the People's Republic of China*, Paris Papers No. 12 (Paris: IRSEM, 2014); On Israel–China relations, see Aron Shai, *Sino-Israeli Relations: Current Reality and Future Prospects*, Memorandum No. 100 (Tel Aviv: Institute for National Security Studies, 2009); Yitzhak Shichor, 'The U.S. Factor in Israel's Military Relations with China', China Brief, Vol. 5, No. 12, Jamestown Foundation, 2005; P R Kumaraswamy, 'At What Cost Israel–China Ties?', *Middle East Quarterly* (Vol. 13, No. 2, Spring 2006).

[52] Robert Art, 'Geopolitics Updated: The Strategy of Selective Engagement', *International Security* (Vol. 23, No. 3, Winter 1998/99).

[53] On the literature discussing isolationism and US foreign policy, see Eric A Nordlinger, *Isolationism Reconfigured: American Foreign Policy for a New Century* (Princeton, NJ: Princeton University Press, 1995); Eugene Gholz, Daryl G Press and Harvey M Sapolsky, 'Come Home, America: The Strategy of Restraint in the Face of Temptation', *International Security* (Vol. 21, No. 4, 1997); Barry R

In unravelling the logic of this extreme hypothesis and imagining a kind of 'East of Suez' scenario for the US military in the Gulf, it is unlikely that another country, even China or India, would be willing or capable to fill this security void. Even if one of the two were to contemplate this kind of ambition, given the tensions within the Asian security complex, an increased military presence from China or India would not produce stability but rather stir local and interregional rivalries.

For all these reasons, the hedging posture of the Gulf countries enables them to diversify their options, but there is no suggestion that leaders in these countries would go as far as to jeopardise their traditional security arrangements. Decision-makers in the Gulf Arab states are fully aware that a power transition from the US to China may end up with Beijing distancing itself from regional issues and avoiding the role of offshore balancer previously played by Washington. A revealing illustration of this Chinese strategic restraint in the Gulf is its consistently neutral position regarding the disputes between GCC members and Iran, or more recently between Saudi Arabia and Qatar. Following the Saudi-led blockade of Qatar in June 2017, the Chinese Ministry of Foreign Affairs issued vague statements that depicted both Saudi Arabia and Qatar as 'comprehensive strategic partners', but without delving into more details, and leaving those expecting a bigger China involvement frustrated.[54] China's neglect of the crisis was further evidenced by its decision to sign a security cooperation pact with Qatar in 2017.

In this context, the three cases reviewed in this chapter show the limits of the geopolitical logic of Gulf hedging strategies. If economic exchanges are likely to continue without too many impediments, the strengthening of political ties will eventually raise issues at the regional level, about Iran or the India–Pakistan stand-off, and at the global level, about Gulf traditional reliance on the US security umbrella. Currently, Gulf leaders have no obvious incentive to provoke a sudden realignment, but the volatility of the security environment should not be underestimated: the more the US becomes an unpredictable ally, the more GCC members will look to diversify their strategic options. Incentives to cross the threshold of a strategic realignment may not exist today and they may not even materialise, but from a long-term perspective, the Gulf–Asia rapprochement depicted in this paper only took ten years to form. It may prelude a new chapter in coming years.

Posen, *Restraint: A New Foundation for U.S. Grand Strategy* (Ithaca, NY: Cornell University Press, 2015).
[54] Mohammed El-Said, 'How is China Involved in Gulf Crisis?', *Daily News Egypt*, 17 July 2017.

CONCLUSION

Over the past ten years, Gulf politics have significantly evolved. The uncertainties that surround US policy in the region have triggered a hedging strategy by GCC members. Hedging has been conducted in other places: some European countries have arguably followed a similar approach between the US and Russia, while small states in Asia have also attempted to avoid being trapped in the US–China competition by sustaining political and economic ties with both players. But, as underlined at the beginning of this paper, the politics of the Arabian Peninsula have been under the influence of Western partners for so long that the current emergence of hedging policies in the region may be historically more consequential than it has been for others.

This trend should neither be ignored nor exaggerated. The erosion of US power in the Middle East logically urges local actors to revise their security arrangements, or at least to reconsider their priorities. At the same time, the economics of Gulf–Asian relations are likely to remain the driving force of the rapprochement, especially in the field of energy and infrastructure investment. However, many unknowns remain regarding the extent of these Gulf–Asian ties. Although countries have expressed a general interest in military cooperation, the operationalisation of this intent has been modest for the most part. Military-to-military ties have increased through the launch of diverse exercises and joint training activities, but initiatives that go beyond operational matters to include strategic dialogues and the signing of defence agreements have not yet materialised. If in the near future, Gulf and Asian countries were to give texture to the military dimension of their relations, it would eventually alter their regional security arrangements and stir sensitive issues such as Gulf relations towards Pakistan or Asian exchanges with Iran.

The situation is made even more complex by the current state of Gulf politics. As the previous chapters argued, the Gulf 'pivot' towards Asia is a regional phenomenon, but not a regional policy. The Qatar crisis of June 2017 is a strong reminder of the fundamental disagreements among Gulf monarchies, and of the inability of the GCC to play an effective role as a regional security organisation. Its members barely consult each other on foreign policy matters, and Asian affairs are no exception to this rule. This means that, as in other cases, the Asia policies of GCC countries may eventually conflict and compete with each other. As a result, hedging may be a convenient option for these states in the short term, but in the longer term may not bring stability or a new regional order: Gulf and Asian countries eventually pursue their own national policies without much consideration for regional coherence or coordination.

For policymakers and scholars, the transition experienced by the Arabian Peninsula and portrayed in this paper constitutes a major challenge. For the practitioner, it defies past certainties about Western strategic supremacy in the region. But because hedging is not a definitive balancing act, it does not offer a clearer regional map, only an evolving mosaic of Gulf–Asia relations that engender contradiction as much as cooperation. In other words, it demands government representatives engaging with the Gulf to take stock of this new layer of complexity. In some cases, this could positively pave the way for new diplomatic initiatives involving Western, Gulf and Asian partners, for instance in the field of maritime security in the Indian Ocean.

For the scholar, putting the paradoxes of this Gulf–Asia rapprochement into perspective may require a revision of the traditional theoretical constructs that enabled an understanding of the region. The volatility of this new environment and the absence of multinational coordination obviously complicate the work of revision. As a result, there is a growing need for scholarship that closely takes into account the burgeoning economic, political and military exchanges between countries in Asia and the Gulf to measure the impact of these trends at both regional and global levels. More broadly, what is sometimes referred to as 'South–South relations' – meaning exchanges that exclude Western countries – should no longer be reduced to a mere matter of concern for area specialists, but should be taken into account by the strategists that aim to better grasp the consequences of these trends on the international system.